Inside Outsourcing

Inside
Outsourcing

The insider's guide to
managing strategic sourcing

Charles L. Gay &
James Essinger

NICHOLAS BREALEY
PUBLISHING

LONDON

First published by
Nicholas Brealey Publishing in 2000

36 John Street
London
WC1N 2AT, UK
Tel: +44 (0)207 430 0224
Fax: +44 (0)207 404 8311

1163 E. Ogden Avenue, Suite 705-229
Naperville
IL 60563-8535, USA
Tel: (888) BREALEY
Fax: (630) 898 3595

http://www.nbrealey-books.com

ISBN 1-85788-204-0

British Library Cataloguing in Publication Data
A catalogue record for this book is available from the British Library.

Library of Congress Cataloging-in-Publication Data
Gay, Charles L.
   Inside outsourcing : an insider's guide to managing strategic sourcing /
Charles L. Gay & James Essinger.
      p. cm.
   Includes bibliographical references.
   ISBN 1-85788-204-0
   1. Contracting out. I. Essinger, James, 1957- II. Title.
HD2365 .G39 2000
658.7'2--dc21

99-462085

Printed in Finland by WSOY.

Contents

Preface

Part I What is outsourcing?   **1**

1   OUTSOURCING: THE CONCEPT   2
    The market value of outsourcing   3
    Making businesses more competitive   5
    Types of outsourcing   6
    Why do organizations outsource?   8
    The benefits of outsourcing   11
    The downside   12
    The need to manage outsourcing   16
    Successful outsourcing   17

2   THE GROWTH OF
    STRATEGIC SOURCING   19
    The concept of strategic sourcing   26
    What does the organization do?   30
    Going back to one's roots   36

3   APPROACHES TO OUTSOURCING   37
    Managing service provision in-house   38
    Contracting out activities   41
    Outsourcing the service   41
    Co-sourcing   45
    Benefit-based relationships   46
    Which approach is best for you?   49

Part II Outsourcing in practice   51

4   WHICH APPROACH IS RIGHT
       FOR YOU?   52
       Preliminary investigations   53
       Defining the business case   57
       Conclusion   76

5   ESTABLISHING THE CONTEXT   77
       The internal analysis and evaluation
       process   80
       Research and baseline analysis   83
       Baseline modeling/benchmarking   84
       The benchmarking process   85

6   PLANNING   88
       The nature of the plan   89
       Preparing the plan   91
       Conclusion   105

7   SELECTING THE SERVICE
       PROVIDER   106
       Two models of selecting the service
       provider   107
       The specification of service   108
       Listing potential candidates   118
       Evaluating suppliers   120
       Request for proposals   123
       Supplier contact   125
       The contract management team   126
       Developing the SLA   128
       Communication   129

8   LEGAL ASPECTS OF OUTSOURCING   131
       The memorandum of understanding   132
       The contract   134

Other legal issues 149
Conclusion 150

9   HUMAN RESOURCES 151
Guidelines for managing human
resources 152
Transition plan 159
Stakeholders 161
Focus on the positive 161
Conditions and benefits 162
Employee resistance 163

10 IMPLEMENTATION AND
MONITORING 170
The transition to working with the
service provider 171
The implementation and monitoring
process 173
Common problems 179
Measuring the benefits of outsourcing 181
Reletting the contract 185
Conclusion 188

Appendix: Outsourcing Surveys 189
The Shreeveport survey 189
The Outsourcing Institute Survey 231

Index 237

Preface

Our aim in this book is to give you a true insider's knowledge of outsourcing: a detailed acquaintance with what outsourcing is, why it is regarded as such an important resource, what the rationale for outsourcing ought to be, whether an organization ought to be doing it and, if so, how it should go about it.

As we explain, the adoption of a strategic perspective on outsourcing is today regarded as one of the most useful and important business methodologies, giving organizations the world over the opportunity to liberate their full potential for profitability, efficiency and cost-effective operation, and allowing them maximum flexibility in terms of retaining and broadening their customer franchise.

Adopting this strategic approach to sourcing now plays a key role in the private and public sectors of most of the world's developed countries, and increasingly in many developing ones.

The extent to which organizations adopt the approach *successfully* is another matter. Unfortunately, there is evidence that many who rethink how they handle their sourcing do not get the results they hoped for – in some cases, the outcome does not even remotely resemble those results.

We believe that a sourcing initiative must, above

all, have the clear aim of generating real, measurable benefits for a business rather than simply offloading an area of responsibility. Unfortunately, too many sourcing initiatives wind up simply doing the latter. They may have been started with the intention of achieving the former, but that, all too frequently, isn't what actually happens.

Even in the US, whose organizations spend far more on outsourcing every year than those of any other country, there is often a clearly discernible lack of direction as far as outsourcing is concerned, too hazy a focus on what the real objectives of an outsourcing initiative should be. Many US organizations cling with almost stubborn persistence to the notion that outsourcing is primarily a kneejerk reaction to a business function that is causing too many difficulties when one tries to handle it oneself. 'If it's a hassle, outsource it' is hardly a particularly dignified or coherent management theory, but it is one that is practiced every day in the US and many other countries.

We believe that too many outsourcing initiatives suffer from bad motives from the start, and that even those that do have good motives suffer from a lack of proper planning. Furthermore, even those that are planned properly can end up using the wrong service provider, and even those that make none of these mistakes are often badly managed and even more badly monitored. Billions of dollars, pounds, yen, deutschmarks and francs – to say nothing of roubles, zlotys, forints and dinars – are wasted each year because outsourcing is not handled properly.

In *Inside Outsourcing* we aim – above all – to give you the tools to ensure that the potential benefits of outsourcing are achieved in your organization, rather than remaining precisely that: *potential*.

Many people at Shreeveport have given us access to their expertise, experience and suggestions while we were preparing this book. In particular, we extend our warmest gratitude to, in alphabetical order, Kay Allan, Kevin Bailey, Abhi Barve, Michael Berntson, Tiffani Byrd, Dave Heijmans, Neil Jones, Michael Lennox and Richard Self. We would like to extend special thanks to Polly Newport for drawing on her wealth of experience in some of the most complex outsourcing exercises to provide us with invaluable assistance. Particular thanks are also due to Sally Lansdell for her skilful editing and suggestions for the book.

Charles L. Gay
James Essinger

Part I

What Is Outsourcing?

1

Outsourcing: the concept

Fly British Airways from Birmingham to Berlin and you fly on a BA aircraft, don't you? Actually, you don't.

The plane has the BA livery, the crew wear the BA uniforms and the cabin staff dress in the corporate style, but what you are really traveling on is a service that has been outsourced in its entirety. A Danish shipping company, Maersk, provides the aircraft, crew and cabin staff. The in-flight catering has been outsourced to Gate Gourmet, and the chances are that you bought your ticket through an independent travel agent.

In fact, British Airways is the nearest thing yet to a virtual company. Engineering is outsourced and ground staff work for local companies around the globe. None of these areas is considered by BA to be core to its business. Instead, it focuses on its one true asset, ownership of the customer.

Is this a one-off? Far from it. The Co-operative Bank takes a similar view. Account management, credit card billing, computer records, check clearing, cash handling and automated teller machines are all elements that you would think are core to a bank's business, but not at the Co-operative Bank, where they are all provided by third parties. What the bank focuses on is customer satisfaction, arguing that the interface with the customer is sacrosanct.

A further example is Abbey National, which is in the process of launching a new internet bank where everything is outsourced save the customer interface. In fact, the bank will have just 50 employees, the majority of whom will be engaged in answering telephone queries.

The market value of outsourcing

The London Stock Exchange support services sector, where publicly quoted outsourcing companies such as SERCO and Capita are listed, is now worth £28 billion or 1.8 percent of the All Share Index.

These are two companies that demonstrate the incredible growth of outsourcing in recent years. In the late 1980s when Capita came to the Alternative Investment Market, it had 25 employees and a value of around £3 million. Today, it is worth a staggering £1.7 billion, attained on the back of doing administrative functions for other people.

A similar growth rate is true of SERCO. From its humble origins of providing contract labor to the likes of the European Space Agency and the UK Ministry of Defence in the mid-1980s, it is now a global business with a market worth of £1 billion.

The *Harvard Business Review* identified outsourcing as one of the most important management ideas and practices of the last 75 years. At Shreeveport we define outsourcing as:

✓ the transfer to a third party of the continuous management responsibility for the provision of a service governed by a service level agreement.

defin

✓ More than 90 percent of US companies outsource one or more activities. According to the international business research organization IDC, worldwide spending on outsourcing reached $99 billion in 1998. IDC confidently expects spending on outsourcing to top $150 billion by 2003.

stat

IDC[1] found that, as one might expect, the majority of worldwide spending on outsourcing occurs in the US, the world's largest economy. In 1998, US organizations spent $51.5 billion on outsourcing, almost 52 percent of global outsourcing expenditure.

The 1999 Outsourcing World Summit (coordinated by Dun and Bradstreet) found that the fastest-growing areas for outsourcing worldwide were:

fastest growing areas

+ human resource management
+ media management
+ information technology
+ customer service
+ marketing.

This research found that the countries where the extent of outsourcing was growing most rapidly were:

+ western Europe:
  – UK
  – France
  – Germany
  – Italy
+ China
+ Taiwan
+ Australia.

In sectors such as media and publishing, outsourcing has been a long-established practice. It is normal for publishing houses to use external organizations for data sourcing, design and layout, printing, subscription and distribution services. In contrast, in the pharmaceutical industry outsourcing has only recently been applied in areas such as property management and site services, although there is potential for far more.

Most large companies use other organizations for some services, which may include IT, factoring, debt collection, payroll, claims processing, estate and property maintenance, temporary and contract employees, public relations, cleaning and catering. These may be informal arrangements with services provided when required, or formal deals incorporating contracts or service level agreements.

Making businesses more competitive

For many years organizations have been outsourcing activities without necessarily calling it that. For example, outsourcing of the sales ledger function is common, based on a contingent contract, where the third party earns the bulk of its revenue by its efficiency in collecting outstanding monies. Increasingly, however, outsourcing has pushed its way up the value chain to the point where it has become an option of real strategic importance.

'Outsourcing' is itself a relatively new term and can be applied to many different types of commercial relationships between purchasers and suppliers – co-sourcing, subcontracting, partnering, joint ventures, third-party contracts, facilities management, managed services, management buyouts, strategic insourcing.

Ultimately, outsourcing is merely a way of getting something done. What *is* interesting is how outsourcing enables an organization to run more efficiently and cost effectively, and how it improves the level of productivity throughout an economy as a whole.

Shreeveport is a consultancy that makes extensive use of outsourcing as a methodology in the business solutions it recommends to its clients and implements on their behalf. But Shreeveport is a business and management consultancy, not an outsourcing consultancy. We are interested in outsourcing because it helps to make businesses more competitive, and – even more significantly – it has the potential to introduce a remarkable level of streamlining and extra efficiency in industry and commerce generally. It can enable organizations to attain world-class performance. Like a car's engine, outsourcing makes things happen, but what really matters is who is in the car, where they are heading, and why they are going there.

Types of outsourcing

The main types of outsourcing currently practised by organizations are as follows:

✢ *Contracting out the activities* – an organization delegating to another organization the element of the demand chain in question. Typically, contracting out is used for fairly low-level ancillary services such as cleaning and managing washroom hygiene. This is a short-term, tactical solution, all too often initiated not because the process fits in with the organization's perspective of how it wants to develop strategically, but rather because it needs to find an urgent means of dealing with a problem.

✢ *Outsourcing the service* – carefully selecting and then engaging specialized external service providers who will allow the organization to redefine, refocus and, if necessary, energize that service in order to tap into the expertise that the service provider has accumulated. Properly managed, this enables the organization to benefit from the service provider's contribution at a deep and strategic level, which may ultimately enable it to focus more and more on what it does best and on where it has a real edge over competitors.

✢ *Insourcing* – an alternative approach to securing productivity gains by improving the operation of an area so that work from other businesses can be undertaken. In this way skills can be retained and assets exploited, resulting in low unit costs for the insourcing business. While this does not free up management time, it does provide a way of making a viable business unit out of an activity that may be too small on its own but is too important or difficult to outsource, for whatever reason.

✢ *Co-sourcing* – a relationship where the interaction between the supplier and the host organization is even more intimate than in normal outsourcing. This usually means that the host organization supplies staff or managers to the outsourcing deal, not as transferred staff but because of their specialist knowledge, which the host organization cannot afford to lose permanently. It is not to be confused with managers merely avoiding outsourcing by seeking to retain staff – co-sourcing means both organizations having responsibility for the supply of resources to meet the objective. There is also some risk, since there may be no redress if objectives or targets are not met.

✤ *Benefit-based relationships* – a long-term relationship based on both parties making an up-front investment in the relationship and sharing the benefits as they accrue according to some pre-agreed formula. In this way both parties take a risk and both should share the reward. If the benefits of the relationship do not materialize, then the supplier may not be guaranteed any recompense for their effort/input.

Both co-sourcing and benefit-based relationships are relatively new and are still developing in terms of the way they operate.

Why do organizations outsource?

Organizations have traditionally carried out a wide range of extremely diverse and frequently non-core activities in-house. This was typically because:

✤ there was, at one stage, a perceived benefit to running them in-house – often driven by poor supplier management and bargaining or lack of real competition in service provision (state monopolies or restrictive practices driving up prices)
✤ they came as baggage after an acquisition or merger and the opportunity was not taken for a hard look at their viability
✤ pure size was a goal (often driven by ego), regardless of the actual nature of the operations. French and Japanese banks used to be classic examples of this (and possibly still are), where the only measure used was, in effect, asset size and therefore any operation that increased this was brought into the fold

✤ some degree of vertical integration was pursued as manufacturers sought to control the value chain, often with good intentions at the time – e.g. to ensure the supply of a rare commodity or because they perceived that value was added at different stages and they could therefore improve returns

✤ divisional heads were allowed to build empires without due regard to the true corporate goals and vision. In one UK bank the head of non-banking services created a whole series of businesses within the infrastructure, including sales of furniture and stationery to third parties, until a strategic review realized that this ran counter to the core focus of the bank's operations. The review focused on shareholder value and many of the services were stopped or outsourced.

Changing markets and increasing regulation in many operational areas are now forcing a fundamental reappraisal of such aggregation of activities. This has lead to an increasing shift back to core operations and activities and in some cases further shrinkage of the value chain directly under the organization's control.

For example, Ford and other large car makers are outsourcing sub-systems supplies for their vehicles, everything from suspension to seating. Ford keeps overall responsibility for final assembly, but suppliers of equipment and machine tools become responsible for managing parts of the assembly plant, such as paint shops and body frames.[2] And in 1999 Ford in South America even announced the outsourcing of the entire car.

The Outsourcing Institute[3] claims that the top ten reasons that companies outsource are to:

✢ reduce and control operating costs
✢ improve company focus
✢ gain access to world-class capabilities
✢ free up internal resources for other purposes
✢ obtain resources not available internally
✢ accelerate reengineering benefits
✢ deal with a function that is difficult to manage/out of control
✢ make capital funds available
✢ share risks
✢ obtain a cash infusion.

top ten reasons to outsource [handwritten margin note]

The organizations at the leading edge of changed attitudes towards outsourcing have taken their vision and goals as a strategic backdrop and reevaluated their operational activities against them. This has enabled them to reduce drastically the scale and scope of what they do in house.

This may involve activities previously perceived as fundamental to the business. For example, in one of the largest outsourcing deals in its sector, UK bank The Halifax agreed to outsource all its credit card processing to EDS.[4]

An increasing number of executives see outsourcing as a way to reshape their corporation – to move away from the vertically integrated organizations of the past and create more flexible, focused organizations that rely on outsourcing to enhance their core abilities and optimize relationships with their customers. A recent survey conducted in the UK by the Economist Intelligence Unit revealed that 80 percent of the organizations studied cited a 'flexible organizational structure' as a key success factor in the coming years. More than 40 percent of respondents believed that their organizations will be substantially or fully virtual by the year 2010. Generally, respondents regarded outsourcing as having the same kind of importance as mergers and acquisitions in creating the competitive organizations of tomorrow.

A study conducted by the Warren Company, a consultancy firm based in Rhode Island, makes it clear that there is a definite trend for outsourcing relationships to be increasingly collaborative. Many of these relationships are, in essence, alliances and joint ventures. This trend is being accelerated by the new organizational models being developed by the growth of e-business, where collaboration with different partners in many different ways is a competitive necessity. One thing is certain: during the twenty-first century, an organization's ability to create and sustain such relationships will be essential to success.

The benefits of outsourcing

Shreeveport's survey of the outsourcing practices of large organizations[5] (outlined in detail in the Appendix) found that the main benefits derived from outsourcing are:

+ reduction in the cost of obtaining the service
+ reduction in the headcount of the organization
+ flexibility in terms of service delivery
+ access to expertise
+ improved service
+ extra management time
+ focus on core services
+ improved quality
+ less need for capital investment
+ cash inflow.

We also discovered what we call 'leveraged benefits', those accompanying the implementation of out-sourcing that were not necessarily expected. These include:

✛ acting as a catalyst for change by highlighting the need for improvements elsewhere in the organization
✛ challenging, aiding and supporting other business initiatives such as IT implementations, process modeling and business process reengineering
✛ initiating or fueling cultural change by educating people about creative service delivery options
✛ stimulating critical business analysis because of the requirement to document business processes and their costs
✛ focusing on the costs of services when alternative sourcing becomes a reality
✛ where it is working well, providing a strong case for the introduction of outsourcing to other areas of business
✛ invigorating businesses by converting sometimes sluggish functional areas into dynamic, successful ones and thereby stimulating internal competition and pride.

The downside

Outsourcing doesn't always bring the anticipated benefits, however. A major international study by business researchers from Oxford University's Institute of Information Management and the University of Missouri followed the track record of 29 of the biggest outsourcing deals over the past eight years. The researchers concluded that more than 35 percent of the deals had failed.

The definition of a 'failure' is always open to debate. Nevertheless, the research unquestionably raises important concerns about the success of outsourcing. As the authors report:

Unsuccessful deals shared certain characteristics. Virtually all the failures sought primarily cost reduction. The organizations were in financial trouble and saw total information technology outsourcing as a financial package to improve company position, rather than as a way of leveraging IT for business value, and keeping control of their IT destiny.

Any kind of IT or other outsourcing should be seen as part of an entire strategy to rethink how an organization does business, rather than as a short-term expedient to solve an essentially tactical problem.

The researchers continued:

All [the failures] were 10 to 12-year single-supplier deals, initiated by the company board with little IT management input.

They reported that organizations suffering failures:

incurred significant hidden costs and degradation of service. Power asymmetries developed in favor of vendors, and organizations suffered a loss of control over their IT destiny. They did little to build and sustain client–vendor relationships, but were reluctant to change vendor because of the high switching costs.

And a failure of the whole initiative is not the only problem. In 1998, a study published by KPMG Consulting[6] found that 75 percent of the 123 organizations responding to the survey were dissatisfied with at least one important part of their outsourcing contract, although 90 percent reported that they were satisfied with the general level of service they received.

Too many organizations are engaging in outsourcing initiatives without really knowing what they are doing. Even if they understand why they are embarking on the project (and the majority probably don't), they may not know how to plan it effectively. Even if they know that, they may not be adept at selecting the right service providers to meet their needs. And the list of potential pitfalls could go on.

One of the largest information systems outsourcing arrangements in the UK was ended two years into a ten-year, £344 million contract because it was unable to take account of management changes and restructuring at the outsourcing organization, retailer Sears. The contract was established with Andersen Consulting in 1995 when Sears' then CEO Liam Strong centralized IS and finance functions. After his departure in 1997, the new board opted to decentralize again and leave management of those areas to the individual operating companies.[7]

According to the Outsourcing Institute,[8] ten factors need to be present for outsourcing to be successful:

to be success what ↘

+ understanding company goals and objectives
+ a strategic vision and plan
+ selecting the right vendor
+ ongoing management of the relationships
+ a properly structured contract
+ open communication with affected individuals/ groups
+ senior executive support and involvement
+ careful attention to personnel issues
+ near-term financial justification
+ use of outside expertise.

Generally, the main problems experienced in relation to outsourcing all fall under the umbrella of 'failure to achieve benefits'. These include:

+ a failure to achieve expected cost reductions
+ an overall reduction in the quality of a function previously managed in-house
+ a failure to develop a true collaborative relationship with the service provider(s)
+ disputes between the organization and the service provider, particularly in connection with quality of service and levels of remuneration
+ a failure to exploit the opportunities provided by the outsourcing initiative to reach new levels of focus on customer needs and operational flexibility directed at meeting those needs.

The fact that an outsourcing initiative can easily bring problems rather than benefits demonstrates that it is no good for an organization simply to embark on the initiative and hope that everything will turn out as planned. As with any area of business, a successful – or, to envious eyes, 'lucky' – organization creates its own luck by doing things right from the outset. While one can never be certain of exactly how a major new initiative in business is likely to succeed, one can reduce the number of uncertain variables by planning everything properly in advance, and by setting specific performance targets for the organization itself and all service providers. In particular, service providers must be selected according to objective considerations relating to such factors as service quality and price, not according to more subjective, woolly, emotive considerations.

Many outsourcing initiatives come to a sticky end because they pay insufficient attention to the importance of the contract with the service provider. A common mistake, for example, is for the organization to assume that it makes sense to allow the service provider to draw up the service provision contract. This practice might be compared to inviting a hungry crocodile to draw up its suggestions for a lunch menu, and then promising to go along with them. In fact, the contract should be drawn up by the organization that is to foot the bill, not the service provider who is going to enjoy a new income stream.

The need to manage outsourcing

Therefore if an outsourcing initiative is to be successful it must be managed with all the intelligence, meticulous attention to detail, care over financial and operational matters, and sensitivity to the need to forge mutually beneficial relationships with other parties that should govern all significant business initiatives. The main reason that Shreeveport decided to write this book is because of our perception – derived from extensive experience of advising organizations after they had embarked on outsourcing initiatives without specialized guidance – that a failure to achieve expected benefits stems from a failure to manage the outsourcing initiative properly.

There are many stepping-stones on the way to the completion of a truly successful outsourcing initiative, and those stones are slippery. If you do slip and fall, you are likely to cause much more damage to your organization – and your career – than simply getting your feet wet.

Successful outsourcing

This book is about how you can avoid slipping. It draws on the expertise of consultants who between them have several hundred years of experience in helping organizations make outsourcing projects work, bringing those organizations the benefits they expected.

We believe that outsourcing is the most potent management tool ever invented for driving efficiency into an organization. We believe that the particular beauty of outsourcing is its deep-down practicality; it isn't a trendy buzzword from the latest management guru's quiver of instant remedies. The power of this tool lies not in its capacity to effect a rapid, instant solution to an organization's problems, but rather in its potential to help the organization rethink its entire way of doing business, even its reason for existing. *Ultimately, outsourcing is much more than just a business tool, it's a new way of thinking about business.*

So *Inside Outsourcing* is above all a book about business. It is also a book about people. Ultimately, there is really no such thing as 'business', but only people working together in order to achieve a common aim. If a business fulfils – and exceeds – its potential, there is a good chance that many of the people working in it will also fulfil – and exceed – theirs.

Unfortunately, the ability to create and sustain successful outsourcing relationships is not something that many executives possess. Only 21 percent of respondents to the Economist Intelligence Unit survey felt that they and their colleagues were ready to manage in such an environment. Outsourcing requires new management skills – from a disciplined selection process to an understanding of the crucially important elements of culture and chemistry that can make or break a relationship.

In this book we aim to give you the theoretical and practical knowledge to make you an expert in managing your organization's outsourcing relationships. We share with you our passionate interest in outsourcing and the Shreeveport methodology, in order to maximize the likelihood that your outsourcing initiative will be not an embarrassing disappointment, but a glorious success.

References

1 IDC, *US and Worldwide Outsourcing Markets and Trends, 1998–2003.*

2 Tim Burt, Nikki Tait and John Griffiths, 'Ford: Nasser's full service', *Financial Times*, August 9 1999.

3 *Survey of Current and Potential Outsourcing End-Users*, The Outsourcing Institute Membership, 1998.

4 George Graham, 'Halifax: Lender outsources credit cards to EDS', *Financial Times*, August 16 1999.

5 Shreeveport Management Consultancy, *Outsourcing: Winning the Benefits, Reaping the Rewards*, 1997.

6 KPMG Consulting, *The Maturing of Outsourcing*, 1998.

7 www.computerworld.com, 11.05.97.

8 *Survey of Current and Potential Outsourcing End-Users*, The Outsourcing Institute Membership, 1998.

2
The Growth of Strategic Sourcing

*O*utsourcing was initially regarded as a tactical solution to a particular problem, often driven by cost dynamics and not really part of a corporate strategy that could be regarded as strategic. Nor was it seen in relation to other ambitious initiatives that the organization might undertake to bring about dramatic improvements in its performance and profitability.

Initial forays into the field now recognized as outsourcing were in the form of the computer bureaux formed in the 1960s. These organizations, such as Baric, Computel and SIA, had a valuable and hard-to-obtain asset – a computer. These computers, fed by punch cards and with much less processing power and memory than we have on a desktop PC today, needed to be housed in special temperature-, humidity- and dust-controlled environments with a small army of operators to tend them. They were too costly to run for the few hours a week that most companies then required, so organizations bought time on others' machines, effectively outsourcing to gain the benefits of investment and specialist skills.

The 1970s saw the expansion of the 'delegation of irksome function' market to cover other ancillary services such as security and catering. It would, however, be misleading to imply that all types of organizations started sourcing these services elsewhere during the 1970s. For example, the Bank of England only began outsourcing its catering function in 1997.

This type of delegation outsourcing bears no real relation to the more strategic outsourcing practised today. A better term to describe the external sourcing of ancillary services on a largely tactical basis is facilities management. This often includes such services as engineering, as well as buildings maintenance (painting, carpentry, wiring and so on).

The new approach to outsourcing that would eventually come to dominate was heralded by a completely new perspective on how organizations handled their information technology requirements. Suddenly, IT became 'flavor of the month' in obsolescence terms. Until then, many organizations had allowed their IT departments to do very much 'their own thing'.

Organizations had been scared into thinking that unless their IT investment was very significant, disaster loomed. This thinking, coupled with an often complete lack of understanding of information technology by senior (non-IT) management, led to enormous growth in IT budgets and levels of manpower. However, the new emphasis on reducing costs in all areas of operation, spurred on by greater levels of competitiveness, put a particular spotlight on IT. This went hand in hand with an increased unwillingness on the part of senior managers to allow their IT departments to 'blind them with science' any longer.

These developments had two main consequences. First of all, IT was often downgraded from a board-level appointment to a more subordinate role within a finance or administrative area. Piecemeal outsourcing, the operation of customer helpdesks and the maintenance of personal computers (PC) started to take off. The days were numbered when organizations took it for granted that the information technology requirement would be met within an in-house department.

In the 1990s, IT came under growing scrutiny and several major service providers pushed to increase their share of the market for outsourced IT services. These providers began to move up the value chain and develop service offerings covering the entire spectrum of IT services. With users suffering from diseconomies of scale and the difficulty of migrating from cumbersome legacy (existing) systems, the service providers' offerings became increasingly attractive and the market grew exponentially.

Alongside these developments, many other organizations had been quietly handling activities on what might be termed an insourcing basis: that is, they would carry out certain key tasks such as processing data and handling administration for other organizations. One example was Mellon Bank in the US, which built up a large business in processing items for other banks, as did GE Capital Bank in the UK. This particular development heralded the outsourcing industry's spectacular move up the volume trading axis as well as across it. Major players such as CSC, EDS, IBM and ICL took on increasingly large multi-dimensional and complex deals that broadened the perspective, as well as the scale and scope, of what could be considered outsourcing.

Organizations started to adopt a much more strategic approach to their use of sourcing, and earlier definitions of outsourcing were no longer adequate to cover the role that outsourcing was now playing in an organization's development. Many national governments – notably those of the UK and New Zealand – drove radical change by encouraging public-sector bodies to adopt private-sector efficiency standards. In many cases, departments within major public-sector divisions were floated off into private organizations.

Hand in hand with this new concept of what outsourcing was, or should be, went a surge in imaginative link-ups between different players, designed to exploit synergies between organizations for their mutual benefit. The success of many of these link-ups had a powerful effect throughout the business world.

For example, an agreement between DuPont and CSC to combine their IT resources was a groundbreaking agreement, with both firms benefiting. It involved more than 2500 staff and was based around the aim of CSC developing a better service for the chemicals industry.

DuPont, CSC and Andersen Consulting

The ten-year, $4 billion alliance between DuPont and its IT partners – CSC and Andersen Consulting – is one example of a co-sourcing arrangement. As discussed in Chapter 1, co-sourcing is the provision of integrated services by multiple suppliers, each with a direct relationship with the purchasing organization. The deal has the following features:

+ There are two prime contracts managed by DuPont.
+ CSC will handle all of DuPont's global information systems and technology infrastructure, including all mainframe, midrange and distributed computing, telecommunications and cross-functional services such as helpdesk and disaster recovery.

✛ Andersen Consulting, under its Business Process Management (BPM) practice area, will develop, implement and manage the chemical and energy software applications for DuPont's petroleum subsidiary, Conoco, and for DuPont's chemical business.

✛ It is DuPont's responsibility to manage CSC and Andersen and their specific areas of performance separately. In some cases, work performed by one company will be in direct support of work handled by another. For example, CSC will manage the technical infrastructure for the applications that Andersen is chartered to support.

✛ Both companies have separate contracts with DuPont, providing a specific set of defined services. At the same time, they will have the right to compete for additional business within DuPont; and to use the capabilities and skills they will gain through this deal to market their services to other companies within the chemical and energy industries.

In essence, DuPont maintains significant control over its IT functions. It continues to oversee contract management, identify internal needs and requirements, handle procurement and manage internal process improvement through its own internal consulting organization CBI (Continuous Business Improvement).

From the outset of the contract, all parties had clearly identified the benefits that would accrue to each organization. From DuPont's perspective, it was the ability to build in flexibility to continue to pursue its objectives of forming more joint ventures and continuing its program of acquisitions and divestments. Having a global, dedicated and responsive IT organization would mean that the integration of new ventures would be that much quicker and allow the organization to focus on its core strengths in the chemical industry. DuPont was clear from the outset that it wished to retain the intelligent customer role in-house to ensure that the contract and its management continued to meet its objectives. To this end, the company has retained 70 senior IT professionals worldwide to act as contract managers. In addition, it has kept 1100 IT employees to look after its R&D systems, issues of security and standards and to act as the procurement agents for future services.

For CSC, the DuPont contract represented an opportunity to grow into a new industry. DuPont provided the launchpad for CSC's highly successful Chemical Oil and Gas Group through the 2600 IT professionals transitioned from DuPont. The expertise has enabled CSC to acquire sector-specific skills that it can transfer to numerous other clients. CSC is also allowed to bid for any further IT projects, although it does not have right of first refusal.

What makes the CSC–DuPont relationship special is the flexibility built into the alliance. Both parties recognize that any relationship will change after its inception. According to DuPont's Global Information Technology Alliance Manager, Frank Conway, 'from the moment you go live things start to change'. Flexibility is critical to meeting these changing needs and realizing that a shared vision is essential to the success of the outsourcing arrangement.

More and more organizations are coming to understand that they can become more successful, and more cost-effective, by tapping into their suppliers' expertise and breadth of activity. Typical ways in which this can happen are as follows:

✢ The organization can benefit from existing relationships or contacts that the supplier may have by virtue of its broad base of activities or its prestige in the marketplace. For example, a supplier of steel may well be able to supply other useful metals; a large transport firm may be able to obtain more efficient and cost-effective access to the cargo section of an airline.

✤ The organization may be able to reduce its costs by benefiting from economies of scale. Economies of scale usually occur for one of three reasons. First, economies arise as a consequence of indivisibilities in the production process – a minimum quantity of inputs is required in order for the function to be capable of being carried out at all. Second, economies may be a consequence of specialization – an organization that can devote all its time to carrying out a particular task (even if the task features several constituent elements) will be far more productive than one that can only devote some of its time to the task. Third, a large scale of operation is often needed to take advantage of better machinery or information technology resources, thereby reducing fixed costs as a proportion of unit costs. For instance, no matter how productive a robot assembly line is, it is pointless to instal one to make just five cars a week, because average costs would be enormous.

✤ The organization may not itself have access to the resource, whether human resources, physical equipment, raw materials or high-quality services.

✤ The organization may have experienced so many problems with trying to undertake the particular demand chain element itself that it has lost confidence in being able to do so. Many organizations, for example, have a poor track record in dealing with customer complaints and queries by telephone, partly because they fail to understand that they need to recruit a completely different type of person to handle customers.

✤ The organization may wish to share financial risk with the supplier. External sourcing frequently enables organizations to offload much or all of the risk associated with carrying out a particular function or activity. An IT outsourcer may buy kit against expected business growth. If the growth does not materialize, this is the outsourcer's problem and the outsourcing organization has not taken the risk. However, some risk-related activities cannot be satisfactorily externally sourced: it is difficult, for example, to imagine how a bank could externally source the risk incurred in the trading room where it deals in securities, although this is not to say that there is no scope for an enterprising external supplier coming up with an appealing arrangement for doing precisely this.

The concept of strategic sourcing

It is impossible to go inside outsourcing, as opposed to skirting the subject superficially, without looking at outsourcing from a strategic perspective. In the past, outsourcing has often been used tactically, as a rapid – and often short-term – solution to a particular need or problem. A large factory that decides to deal with the problem of low staff morale and frequent pilfering in its factory canteen by outsourcing the whole canteen function to a specialized caterer is certainly using outsourcing, but not in any particularly strategic sense. There is not much difference between this kind of outsourcing of an element of ancillary service and merely delegating that service to an external party. To exploit the potential of certain types of sourcing to make the entire business perform better at every level, one needs to practice strategic sourcing.

Strategic sourcing means that an organization works with one or more suppliers in order to effect a significant improvement in business performance.

The growing popularity of adopting a strategic approach to sourcing stems from the simple fact that organizations that do this appear to do well. However, making the most of strategic sourcing is an in-depth, difficult and frequently painful process, as well as often requiring a considerable investment. It is not at all a matter of 'pushing a button' and then getting on with other things. On the contrary, push the button of strategic sourcing and your organization may never be the same again.

Strategic sourcing is only likely to be effective, and bring the desired results, if management is prepared to adopt a completely new perspective on management control. Organizations are more likely to meet their commercial objectives and maximize their success if they direct management control not so much towards controlling inputs, but rather towards focusing on the finished output. They need to start from the top, avoiding preconceptions about how to operate, and say to themselves, 'This is what I want my finished product to be; how can I bring it into being with the greatest efficiency and cost-effectiveness?'

The lack of preconceptions is essential. Again and again, Shreeveport has found that an organization is more likely to fulfill its potential if it is prepared to adopt a revolutionary perspective on how it operates, and especially on how it sources elements of the demand chain. If one is going to seek to obtain the maximum benefit from strategic sourcing, one needs to believe in this approach wholeheartedly. That requires courage, energy, hard work and money. But generally, organizations taking that step are delighted with the results, because the benefits far outweigh the input.

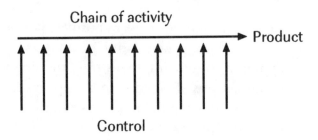

Figure 2.1 *The old model of management control*

Figure 2.1 shows the traditional, 'linear' model of management control. There is a chain of activity, leading to a finished product, and management control is effected at numerous points along the chain. There is no question of the different resources used within the chain of activity being controlled externally; they may originate externally, but control is exercised on them once they have been brought directly within the organization's sphere of influence, and this will frequently involve a physical transfer of the resource into the organization's premises.

Figure 2.2 depicts a completely different model of management control. Here, the organization has adopted a strategic, dynamic approach to sourcing, and has identified, and signed agreements with, various suppliers with which it has decided to work, in order to tap into their expertise to improve business performance to a significant degree.

In this second model, the supplier can be seen as located in the middle of a spider's web, with the suppliers located on the outer rim. The organization's managers remain continually in touch with every supplier. The strands of the web reaching out from the spider to the perimeter are held in a condition of tension, representing the ongoing working relationship between the organization and the suppliers.

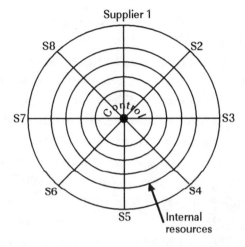

Figure 2.2 *The new model of management control*

Strategic sourcing is not just a matter of tapping into a supplier's expertise, it is also a matter of insulating oneself from a supplier's problems. If you are managing by the traditional model illustrated in Figure 2.1, this insulation is not possible.

Strictly speaking, the spider's web represents the base of a cone, with the finished product being situated on the tip of the cone. This is shown in Figure 2.3. This cone model emphasizes how the activities

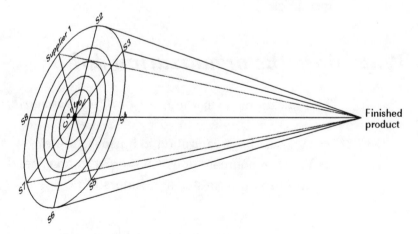

Figure 2.3 *The finished product*

of the various suppliers focus on and converge on the finished product.

It should be clear from the above discussion that there is a huge difference between strategic sourcing and delegation. In delegation, one basically delegates a responsibility to someone or some organization and then lets them get on with it. The person or organization involved will have no real interest in the other organization once its own responsibilities have been fulfilled. In strategic sourcing, the supplier works with the organization as a partnership to help it develop its business. The supplier will be aware that its commercial success and future will be intimately bound up with that of the organization it is supplying. In many agreements, the supplier will benefit financially from the organization's increased success.

Furthermore, in the best strategic sourcing relationships, organizations look to their suppliers to provide advice: that is, to be proactive in their supply rather than merely reactive. No manager can seriously expect to know everything there is to know about his or her industry. Suppliers are becoming innovators rather than mere providers of resources.

What does the organization do?

Two questions lie at the heart of *Inside Outsourcing*:

✤ What is the organization in business to do?
✤ What resources does the organization need in order to do what it is in business to do?

What is the organization in business to do?

Answering this question, which on the face of it should be easy, does in fact lead organizations to undertake some complex and interesting thinking. It has to be answered not by pointing to a tangible product or service, *but rather by focusing on a benefit that it offers its customers.*

An organization producing typewriters in the 1960s that had as its corporate purpose the production of typewriters would have gone out of business as soon as demand switched from typewriters in the 1970s and 1980s and instead moved to wordprocessors. On the other hand, a typewriter-manufacturing organization with the perception to see that it was not, fundamentally, in the business of making typewriters, but rather selling its customers the benefit of document production, would have realized that it had to make the transfer to wordprocessors. This is precisely what IBM did with its Display Writer, which then gave way to the PC.

At first sight, many pharmaceutical companies are apparently 'winning the permission of the marketplace' – gaining and retaining customers who 'permit' their suppliers to succeed by buying from them – by selling drugs developed by their in-house research and development teams. However, the real nature of their marketplace permission could in fact be argued to derive from their ability to win customer confidence by linking the drugs with their good reputation. This can be demonstrated by considering the fact that some pharmaceutical companies entrust their research and development to an external organization, albeit with extremely stringent confidentiality and intellectual property agreements governing the relationship.

Sainsbury's Bank

In the mid-1990s, many leading UK retailers – especially supermarkets – moved into the provision of banking services. Safeway, Sainsbury and Tesco all offer banking services as a major part of their activities. Sainsbury's has even formally set up its own bank. When these initiatives were launched, there was considerable discussion in the business press about how this could be the beginning of the end for many traditional banks and that the financial muscle of the retailers, coupled with their expertise and experience at knowing what customers wanted and providing it, would surely spell the demise of many traditional banks, or even of the entire traditional banking sector.

It is important to bear in mind that the retailers are usually buying in banking services from a traditional bank and branding them in order to deliver them to their customers via their retail outlets. Even Sainsbury's Bank relies heavily on banking services provided by the Bank of Scotland. The importance to Sainsbury's of choosing the right banking partner for its new venture is seen in its inviting 40 traditional institutions to tender for the job. Richard Chadwick, deputy chief executive of Sainsbury's Bank, said that the partnership with the bank eventually chosen is a 'joint venture': it might best be seen as a form of co-sourcing rather than outsourcing. He added: 'We were looking for a business partner which was a true cultural fit to our own organization: that is, it had to be in tune with our need for developing an energetic and dynamic bank that would be seen to set a trend for innovation and developing customer-winning services.'

What resources does the organization need in order to do what it is in business to do?

Once the organization has focused on what provides customers with value, it must assess the resources needed to supply this value. Around these resources and the processes they perform will be other, less direct impacts on value. It may be valuable to examine whether less direct value-adding services, or even value-adding services that are currently being poorly performed, could be outsourced.

It is essential for the organization to avoid being over-prescriptive when it starts talking to specific suppliers. Rather than telling suppliers precisely what it wants and specifying every aspect of what it believes itself to need, it should give suppliers freedom to produce the supply required in the most effective way, given their expertise and resources.

This approach requires the organization to be something of a visionary. It has to be prepared to rethink how it will use the element of the demand chain in question and what that element should be. The organization may even have to redesign its entire operation so as to make the most of the specialized expertise, experience, economies of scale and other advantages that its suppliers can offer it. This, as we have seen, is what strategic sourcing is all about.

Above all, the ultimate output must remain paramount. Everything has to be geared around producing it, and around keeping careful track of anything that might cause the customer's needs to change.

What does all this mean at a practical level? Organizations that believe in adopting a flexible and dynamic approach to sourcing are increasingly basing their activities around a hierarchical structure differentiating between the core activity of maintaining relationships with customers, important business processes, and a third grade of activity best described as ancillary services. This hierarchy is shown in Figure 2.4.

The first level of the hierarchy is the relationship with the customer. This is the 'core' activity of an

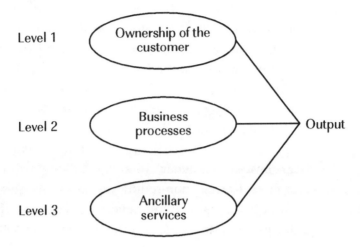

Figure 2.4 *The three-tier supply hierarchy*

organization determined to make the most of the advantages obtainable from strategic sourcing. The relationship with the customer is the one privilege that is truly unique to the organization and that none of its suppliers, however important they might be to its overall operation, can usurp. The relationship with the customer is the edge that matters. The customer extends a franchise to the organization that may be revoked if the organization does not continue to deliver a satisfactory customer value proposition. Whatever else may be sourced from a supplier, the organization must never attempt to outsource its customer franchise.

Amazon

There are many examples of organizations that have in effect decided to control only their customer franchise. Amazon, the internationally successful online bookshop, is essentially only in the business of establishing relationships with customers. It does maintain rigorous control over its distribution – the company planned to open seven warehouses around the US by the end of 1999, involving more than three million sq. ft of warehouse space at a cost of about $200 million. This is the first distribution network designed specifically for online retailing, sending merchandise out item by item to individual customers. It can be seen as contributing to Amazon's core activity, maintaining and controlling its customer franchise. Everything else is secondary. Note, however, that Amazon has still to make a profit: internet companies have something of a history of building up an excellent customer value proposition, and high market capitalization, without actually being profitable.

We describe the second level of the hierarchy as 'business processes'. This describes resources that play an obviously key role in the organization's success. These success-defining resources would include such crucial functions as information technology, raw materials, financial services, accounting, human resources, treasury (i.e. managing cash as an asset) and so on.

There is no entirely objective criterion rigorously defining whether a function belongs in this second tier. The only useful distinguishing point appears to be that functions belonging at this second level of the hierarchy do not feature any intrinsic limit on the benefit that the business can gain from them. The better the quality of the supply, the more the organization is likely to be successful.

This is not the case with the third type of supply, which can be regarded as a necessary evil. There are strict limits to the benefit the business can gain from these functions. Typical examples of such third-tier supplies would be security, cleaning, payroll management, catering and the provision of stationery.

Some commentators use the term 'chore' to describe functions in this third tier. 'Core' and 'chore' are obviously useful polarizations, but unfortunately most analyses fail to give sufficient weight to the second, middle, tier of the hierarchy.

Going back to one's roots

Ultimately, an organization that strives to focus on its core relationship with its customer and uses outsourcing to achieve this end is in effect striving to go back to its roots as an organization.

For example, over the years NASA (the US National Aeronautics & Space Administration) gradually grew its activities into a range of telemetry and tracking facilities. These facilities are now outsourced to Lockheed Martin as part of the CSOC (Consolidated Space Operations Contract) deal. This has enabled NASA to refocus on its core business of running space programs.

Unquestionably, even 20 years ago any rigorous analysis of the structure and means of operation of the vast majority of organizations would have revealed that they devoted surprising, even alarming, amounts of time and energy to functions that had nothing to do with their core activity, the activity that had won them their customer franchise. Now successful organizations are directing their activities towards meeting and broadening their customer franchise in order to win more customers and providing more to its existing ones. This does not necessarily mean that every non-core service should be outsourced, but it certainly does imply that the organization's sourcing must be directed ultimately towards facilitating a greater focus on the customer relationship.

3
Approaches to Outsourcing

An organization wanting to make the most of the opportunities offered by outsourcing should seek above all to capitalize on the benefits offered by new approaches to strategic sourcing. The essence of these benefits, as we have shown, involves the organization tapping into the expertise of the service provider, and frequently also sharing risks with them.

We have depicted outsourcing as, strictly speaking, only one type of approach to strategic sourcing, but nonetheless such an important one that there is considerable justification for making the two terms synonymous. We do so in this book, mainly because 'outsourcing' is a much better-known term worldwide than the more technical 'strategic sourcing', and it seems pedantic not to use it.

In Shreeveport's experience, the term 'outsourcing' is often used generically whereas in fact there are a number of different outsourcing models. In principle, each strategic sourcing exercise is unique; each has different requirements that in turn will determine the optimum solution. Each of the principal models of strategic sourcing or outsourcing is explored in detail below, beginning with a brief summary of another potential option that is often overlooked – retaining the service in-house.

Managing service provision in-house

Outsourcing is an essential tool in managing the plethora of activities necessary to make businesses function successfully. Many organizations find that as they grow these functions are provided in-house. Internal service provision is therefore a viable approach. However, on countless occasions failure to manage the provision of internal services successfully is the overriding reason for making the decision to outsource. This is invariably because the organization has not formally defined the responsibilities of its internal service organizations, who their customers are or what their contribution is to the success of the company.

Signet

Signet, a high-street jewelry chain (previously Ratners), provided its IT operations, support and development internally. When a group of senior managers were asked what requirements they had of the IT unit, they produced a wish list that bore little relationship to what was actually provided or what the unit was capable of providing and, even more fundamentally, what the unit thought its targets were. With such a lack of clarity, it is no surprise that the IT department was criticized at every opportunity.

The success of managing services in-house therefore depends on gaining consensus about what the objectives of the organization and therefore the service are, the targets and measures by which the achievement of these objectives will be measured and the way in which relationships in achieving those objectives are measured.

Our experience of over 150 exercises involving a decision about whether or not to outsource has shown us that the critical success factor is formalizing the relationships surrounding service provision. It is currently very fashionable to review the measures and targets associated with a business endeavor on the basis of 'what gets measured gets done'. While this is true of in-house service provision, who actually does the measuring and of what are critical issues.

In the Signet example, and in many others relating to IT departments, there has historically been a lack of clarity about who was the prime customer of the department. But what is the definition of the customer? It may be that the customer is best defined as the department or individuals who receive the benefit of the service. However, if we take retailing as an example, this also implies that the customer has the money with which to pay. Such a simple approach has profound implications lending clarity to the relationship of service provision: the customer has money that he or she pays when the service is received satisfactorily.

However, this simple philosophy is often lost because of the way the organization is structured. Quite often the customer does not have the money! Or, to put it another way, the person or unit with the money may not be the sole, primary or principal recipient of the service – they may be acting as guardians for the organization and seeing that the service is delivered. The budget may be held 'centrally' and drawn down as needed to fund the service.

The unit managing the budget may be removed from other customers in terms of its priorities and objectives, so a service that seems adequate to that unit may be woefully inadequate to others.

A variant is when the unit providing service holds the budget; in terms of our retail customer this means that the shopkeeper has the money and the goods; or, if you prefer, think in terms of gamekeeper and poacher. You ask for what you want and if you're lucky you may get it, or you may get something different that the shopkeeper thinks will suit you and is more convenient for them to provide. You have no sanctions if you don't like it – you cannot refuse to pay because the shopkeeper already has the money. Because of this you may find that after a while you don't even bother to complain, so the shopkeeper is unaware of the depth of your dissatisfaction.

This can be how internal relationships develop, with poor communication on both sides leading to a growing gap. Formalizing the relationship can help avoid this. A service level agreement (SLA) defining the service required, its outputs and how they will be measured can improve poor service, but it can seem like a lot of bureaucracy for internal departments to go through. There may remain difficulties with services whose customers are a broad group and cannot exercise a 'market response' to the service provided. For example, facilities management provision needs to satisfy the relevant manager, as well as all staff affected by the service. If staff do not like the menu in the canteen, they can bring sandwiches or seek alternative outlets. However, if staff are unhappy with, say, the cleanliness of the building, they cannot go elsewhere.

Contracting out activities

Contracting out happens when external organizations are retained to undertake activities that were
previously done in-house. Traditionally this has often
meant cleaning and catering; that is, it has usually
been restricted to ancillary services. In recent years,
contracting out has developed to include building
maintenance and the range of activities that have
become known as facilities management.

Initially, this approach concerned getting external
organizations to carry out a specific function and
contracts often focused on activities rather than
results. This meant that arrangements were frequently unsatisfactory and those managing contracts
could not understand why quality was poor, in particular because a key element of outsourcing was frequently cost reduction. Where there is a focus on cost
reduction and on activity rather than result, there is
almost always an irreconcilable conundrum. The only
apparent way of improving quality when activities
have been specified is to do more of that activity –
more cleaning to remedy a lack of cleanliness.
However, that will be more expensive. It became evident from contracts let in this manner that a more
sophisticated method of contracting was necessary.

Outsourcing the service

In Shreeveport's experience, if there is one essential
element common to the success of an outsourcing
exercise, it is a definition of the results or outputs or
outcomes that the client organization seeks. To continue the example used above, the approach to outsourcing a cleaning service would be to define the

level of cleanliness required, permitting the supplier to undertake whatever activities are necessary to achieve that level of cleanliness. It is, if you like, a shift from *how* things are done to *what* needs to be achieved. This means that client organizations can be far more confident in outsourcing more complex services.

To recap the discussion in previous chapters, organizations outsource for various reasons, including:

✛ cost reduction
✛ improving service quality
✛ gaining expertise that is difficult to acquire or retain, in particular in functions such as IT that require ongoing training and development
✛ using other organizations' investment capability
✛ exploiting economies of scale
✛ encouraging management focus on core activities.

For successful outsourcing there needs to be clarity about which of these reasons is the most compelling. The most critical difference in addressing these through outsourcing as opposed to contracting out activities is the definition of what is to be achieved.

Outsourcing must therefore focus on the definition of the requirement and the measures by which the success of the outsourcing and therefore the supplier will be measured. This can be an almost impossible task for many organizations. The most obvious group to undertake the definition of what outputs are needed may seem to be the staff and managers currently involved in delivering the function or service, but this poses a number of problems. First, they may be the very staff whose jobs, prospects and pensions are seen as under threat and yet they are being asked to assist in the process. Second, they may also find it difficult to think about the results of their service in an objective way. A supplier could offer to do things differently to achieve the same result, which existing staff often see as implicit criticism. The logic runs as follows:

1 If things could be done better, that implies that the current staff and services are poor.
2 We (as the staff of the function) have had reasonable appraisals/assessments or no major criticism in the past (perhaps management has been encouraging and positive rather than demotivating staff with criticism).
3 Therefore the way we have been doing things must be OK.
4 Therefore we can ask a supplier to do things in the same way and the client organization will be satisfied that they will get good service.
5 If we need to ask suppliers to do something different, then we haven't being doing OK. Why should we bother helping a company that is so ungrateful?
6 Anyway, suppliers can't do the job as well as us because only we know the culture, the managers, what people really want, how to get round the system...

So the primary motivations for embarking on the outsourcing initiative in the first place – reasons such as gaining access to economies of scale, gaining expertise, reducing costs – can be scuppered if the requirements and measures are not defined in terms of outputs. And people genuinely find it hard to convert activity-based thinking (how we do it) into outcome-based definitions (what we want to happen).

Management may not help here either. 'What we want to happen' is probably not what happens now, otherwise why outsource at all? Those reasons for outsourcing are crucial – do managers want lower costs, better quality of service, to stop losing staff and having to train new ones? Within each of these reasons there needs to be better definition – which costs can be lower? What about the link between costs and quality? Eventually lower and lower costs will mean a cheap service, which will have an impact on quality. What about next year, the following year and the year after that – do costs have to keep reducing and reducing? Is that really practicable?

Outsourcing a service therefore involves identifying the need to change beyond what can be achieved in-house, defining the requirements in terms of outputs, outcomes or results, and giving suppliers freedom to respond with how they would achieve those outcomes. It also means understanding very clearly how the remaining organization will function with the outsourced service and an external supplier managing what has previously been 'our own'.

This new relationship will be bounded and defined by a contract. Each party appoints a contract manager (sometimes called a service delivery manager by the supplier) to ensure that the contract is adhered to and that the relationship is running well. However, one difficulty with any relationship bounded by a contract is that the inevitable changes can be major issues. Change can also be an area where both parties feel vulnerable and exposed. This is particularly true of the client organization, which having entered into a contract may feel that its bargaining power when requesting changes is diminished. Past practice has illustrated the vulnerability of client organizations at this point – business 'bought' at a very low price by suppliers, and margins recovered later under the guise of 'change control'.

Many parties in outsourcing are well aware that this is a very short-term approach to developing what is often a major relationship with long-term potential. Increasing requirements for reference sites before entering into a contract also enable clients to check the supplier's approach to the relationship.

Nonetheless, there is clearly the opportunity for a more sophisticated relationship that goes some way to avoiding the problems of change.

Co-sourcing

Co-sourcing is where the relationship between supplier and host organization involves the host supplying – not transforming – some of the people resource to undertake the activity.

BBC

The BBC set up an outsourcing relationship to run its customer service call center. However, because of the detailed knowledge required to answer some of the public's queries on specific subjects of television or radio programs (e.g. if there has been a program dealing with spousal abuse the call operators should be prepared to give advice to distressed callers), the BBC did not want to transfer the staff to the new supplier. These staff were therefore to be retained by the BBC, with the suppliers providing all the infrastructure for call handling and knowledge-based systems to enable the staff to do the job.

Co-sourcing involves working in partnership in a very real sense, because the parties come together as more or less equal partners. For the partnership to work successfully there must be regular contact between people from both the client organization and the supplier at all levels.

The requirements that each party is looking to meet can be met, or a successful compromise reached, if good relationships are maintained, provided that each party understands the other's abilities, needs and aims. As with any partnership some fundamental elements are required, including a good contract, appreciation of the client needs and those of the supplier, and a willingness to satisfy common desires.

This type of relationship is difficult to construct and has to be carefully managed. It has two principal pitfalls. First, it is important that managers in the host organization are not allowed to use or instigate this kind of contract to avoid an ordinary outsourcing arrangement and protect 'their' staff. In some circumstances it is hard enough to get managers to recognize that they can identify affected staff and rely on the outsourcers to supply services effectively without creating the opportunity for even more evasion by using a co-sourcing arrangement.

Second, if both parties are supplying something for the contract goals to be met, there is a risk that no one will be fully accountable if the objectives are not achieved. It is therefore essential to have clear measures of the supplier's performance that enable good contract management to happen, regardless of whether staff have been available or not.

Benefit-based relationships

In this approach the supplier and the host organization both invest in the outsourcing exercise and both share in the rewards. The essence of these relationships is that both organizations agree a baseline and then work together to meet key improvement objectives. Once achieved the benefits are shared between both parties – usually with the host organization getting the majority of the benefits initially and the supplier organization receiving a larger share as more benefits are reaped; as things improve greatly, the supplier organization obtains the lion's share of any further benefits. To achieve this there must be a true trusting partnership or there will be a sense that too much is being gained by the other party. It also requires proper analysis of the metrics – if these are not unequivocal, disputes may ensue. Proper metrics will mean that there should be no disputes about who had which idea and who deserves the benefit. It should be clear that once the benefits are delivered the sharing follows.

Rolls-Royce/EDS

EDS follows this model for business improvement projects in its IT outsourcing arrangement with Rolls-Royce. However, it stresses that the distribution of benefits must be agreed up front and once the project is complete EDS should get its share. The implication of this is that Rolls-Royce must ensure that it implements the business processes that the project recommends, or it will not have the resources to justify paying EDS's share.

In this approach both parties must have complete clarity about the benefits that each is seeking from the relationship. In practice, in order to achieve this each has to make a considerable investment before not just a contract but even an agreement has been reached. The greatest clarity tends to be around the benefits that the client organization is seeking, as it is in this organization that the most confusion may exist about the purposes of a new working relationship with an external organization.

Furthermore, the purposes of the relationship must be defined not just in terms of generic phrases, e.g. reducing costs or improving service, but in a way that allows these purposes to be turned into measurable objectives. In order for these objectives to make sense, they have to be couched in terms of the business strategy that the client organization is pursuing. Therefore if a client organization is pursuing an aggressive growth path and is seeking a partner to manage its entire IT provision, there needs to be clarity on how the supplier partner can control IT management in a way that will contribute to the client organization's growth. The more direct this impact, the clearer the benefit relationship will be.

Where the function that the partner is taking over will have only an indirect impact on the client organization's achievement of its business strategy, then the benefits may have to be defined according to a series of 'value proposals'. Here the supplier takes responsibility for achieving specific, well-defined goals that can be measured in the relatively short term. It must be agreed in advance that achieving the goal will be beneficial to the client organization and for some value to be set on that benefit, even though it may not be possible to measure it directly.

Benefits must also be defined for the supplier organization. It is usually clearer that the supplier is seeking a profitable relationship and one that offers reference site value (i.e. the client organization can be referred to as a success story for the supplier and may be willing to host visits from the supplier organization's potential clients).

Which approach is best for you?

Each of the different approaches to involving a supplier in taking responsibility for part of your business
has different characteristics. Contracting out may be
appropriate when you need to have control of the
process but require additional resources to do it.
Outsourcing provides you with a means of defining
the outputs, or preferably outcomes, and managing a
relationship to ensure that they are achieved. The
process to make the outcome happen is no longer of
interest to you. Co-sourcing and benefits-based relationships will provide you with added extras, but
should be embarked on when you are already a fairly
sophisticated outsourcing manager, as they are more
complex both to define and to manage.

There is no 'one size fits all' outsourcing deal but
a range of approaches that you need to explore to
decide on the one that will be of greatest added value
to your business.

Part II

Outsourcing in Practice

4
Which Approach Is Right for You?

*T*his chapter gives practical information to help you make a decision about whether your own organization should be gaining the strategic (and, to a lesser extent, tactical) advantages of outsourcing. Of course, our ability to provide this information is limited, in the sense that the advice in a book cannot relate to specific cases. However, Shreeveport's experience is that there are many important guidelines relating to the outsourcing decision itself, just as in subsequent chapters of this part we present other guidelines relating to the successful implementation of an outsourcing initiative.

If the discussion so far in this book has whetted your appetite for how outsourcing might be able to give your own organization (whether you own it or work for it) access to unprecedented levels of profitability and efficiency, you will certainly be wondering how you can decide whether outsourcing is right for your organization.

One way of deciding whether outsourcing is right for you would be to do it and see what happens. This might be termed the 'suck it and see' principle.

Sucking something and seeing what happens is all very well if you've chosen a soft-centered chocolate or a fresh strawberry. However, if you've chosen something less palatable, you run the risk of ending up with an approach similar to that of Victorian chemists, who convinced themselves that an important way to analyze a chemical was to taste it. Not surprisingly, this advice is not at all sensible if the chemical chosen is noxious. And given modern agriculture's heavy use of pesticides, what seems like a fresh strawberry may turn out to have consequences not at all to your liking.

Preliminary investigations

An outsourcing initiative is only likely to work if it has first been the subject of thorough investigation. Unfortunately, carrying out a thorough investigation will not guarantee that the initiative succeeds, but it is unlikely that the initiative will work without that detailed thinking and planning. Quite apart from anything else, the thorough investigation should reveal potential problems with the entire outsourcing concept and may cause a more outlandish outsourcing scheme to be scuppered before it reaches the light of day.

The more preliminary thinking and decision making that is done, the better – provided that a decision is actually made and action actually taken. Almost by definition, outsourcing is a 'hands-on' management function. There is no room in an outsourcing initiative for the ivory tower thinker, and the last thing an organization should be doing is preparing a flimsy report to be submitted to the members of the board, who may rubber-stamp it without having any idea of what they are really doing.

All options should be carefully considered, ranked against an agreed set of criteria, and then weighted according to risk. This should provide a well-evaluated and carefully considered conclusion that is likely to provide a reliable idea of whether the initiative will work.

Typical questions that need to be answered in detail are as follows.

What is the purpose of the exercise?

It is close to impossible to make an outsourcing initiative work if you don't know why you are doing it. You need to be certain about the fundamental motivation: is it to reduce costs? Improve quality or performance? Remove a thorn in the side of the organization? There may be more than one motive, and it is important to remember that different people might see the motives in a different light, in the same way that different people have different views about movies or books. However, it should be possible to reach some kind of consensus on motivation. And it hardly needs to be added that this motivation needs to tie in with the organization's commercial objectives.

Ultimately, it should be obvious that for any decision it is necessary to be clear about why it is being taken. If the objectives arising from the decision are not clearly stated, well understood and agreed by all parties from the outset, then it will not only be almost impossible to capture the benefits, but there is also likely to be fundamental disagreement as to the outcomes. Different objectives require different approaches, and will also lend themselves to different contracts, different risk profiles and different timescales.

What is the service or function being considered for outsourcing?

Answering this question means defining the boundaries or scope of the service or function with considerable (though not inflexible) clarity. Obviously, this definition will be absolutely essential if and when the initiative progresses to the stage of shortlisting and then selecting a vendor. It is clearly impossible to get a service provider to quote for providing a certain function unless they know what they are supposed to be doing.

Even more to the point, an organization can hardly make any assessment of whether outsourcing a particular service or function is likely to succeed unless it has a precise idea of what constitutes the service or function. Another important point here is that if a lack of clarity pervades this initial, crucial decision, it is all too likely to infiltrate into agreements drawn up with service providers and lead directly to debates over whether something should have been included in the agreement or not, and the level of quality to which it should have been delivered.

Does the organization have a compelling need to undertake the outsourcing initiative?

At first sight this may seem a tautologous question, because the whole purpose of the decision-making process is supposed to be to answer this very point. But while it is necessary for the overall decision-making process to be meticulous and wide-ranging, this does not mean that the decision must be cold-blooded. Consider a decision to get married – anybody who based that decision on a spreadsheet featuring different percentages relating to the other person's advantages and disadvantages would, with reason, be regarded as a crank. If there is no fundamental enthusiasm the marriage is not going to work, even if the spreadsheet analysis is favorable. Similarly, outsourcing is such an enormous change for an organization that it cannot possibly be considered lightly. Nor can it be undertaken without passion and determination to make it succeed.

It is also important to note that while there may be no compelling need for this particular function to be undertaken, in the larger context there may be a compelling reason for a range of functions to be outsourced, of which this one is merely a small part. The whole may therefore subsume the smaller elements, even if it may be counter-intuitive when considered in isolation. For example, there may be a good reason to outsource legacy systems in a firm as well as, say, desktop support and the helpdesk function. But the deal may be much more favorable to both parties – and especially to the organization doing the outsourcing – if more activities are included such as development or enhancement of other systems.

In addition, where the decision has been made in principle to outsource activities, it will still be necessary to obtain the sanction of senior-level decision makers. They will question the need and the benefits. It is therefore important to present such a compelling business case that their acquiescence can be assured.

Does this initiative have direct relevance to our overall strategic intentions?

Once the compelling need for outsourcing has been established, the ostensible goals and objectives of the potential initiative must be examined and considered objectively. Above all, they must be appraised in relation to the organization's strategic intentions.

Perhaps the most important question of all is: 'Does this potential initiative have direct relevance to our overall strategic intentions as an organization?'

If the answer to this question is not yes, why are you considering outsourcing at all?

If the answer is yes, the next stage is to consider all the following questions:

✢ Is our objective clear?
✢ Have all the options been identified?
✢ Has data been gathered to explain:
  – the impact of proceeding with each of the options under consideration
  – the risk of proceeding with each of the options under consideration
  – the likelihood of the risks occurring
  – the cost of proceeding with each option
  – the timings relating to each option
  – the implications of *not* proceeding with the option (this requires particularly careful consideration)?

Defining the business case

After the initial investigation but before any positive decision can be made to go down the outsourcing road, a business case has to be set out for it. This must cover both financial and non-financial issues. Frequently what happens in practice is that the person who had the idea in the first place assumes a kind of messianic role in order to spread the word. Certainly, that person needs to be able to convince all other influential people in the organization – the older people, the entrepreneurial type, those who prefer to follow orders but who nonetheless may be highly effective, and of course those who pull the strings financially – that the outsourcing initiative is a worthwhile route to take.

The financial case for proceeding with the outsourcing initiative needs to be especially persuasive and compelling.

Business case example

For example, in a large manufacturing organization, the IT function did not support the business effectively. IT support, supply and maintenance were fragmented, with each of the many business units having their own services, in different structures, with their own budgets. There was no IT or information systems strategy. There were many different versions of software and hardware, and different products to do the same thing in different business units. The company was not consistently connected to e-mail.

However, the company as a whole was in a shrinking market and needed to streamline existing activities and diversify into new business areas to survive and thrive. A compelling need arose to 'do something' about IT and that 'something' became to outsource it! A project team was assembled – there was no in-house expertise in outsourcing. What could be done?

At this stage outsourcing was a concept owned by the project team – it was their *raison d'être*. There was no business case in the sense of cost–benefit analysis, only a feeling, verging on certainty, that outsourcing would be better. Then the project stalled because of a lack of senior management commitment.

On arriving at the company, Shreeveport consultants immediately did two things. We started to make a plan (more of that later) and we began to develop the business case. The basis of this consisted of an analysis of current costs and service, a hypothesis, based on research and experience, of what an outsource provider could do to make it better, and a study of the risks.

There were two difficulties in developing the business case. First, there was very little known and documented about current IT provision in terms of costs, service levels, numbers of staff involved and items of software and hardware held. So we did not know anything quantifiable about the current situation and there were no investment plans.

Secondly, at this very early stage we did not know for certain what an outsourcing supplier would offer in terms of savings or service improvements and how this balance would affect price and quality.

So we had to build a business case when we did not know the costs and had to guess the benefits. No problem!

The essential at this stage was to move the project away from the 'messiah of outsourcing' phase to a sound financial and service quality footing – do this and that and things will get better.

We therefore worked at getting an estimate of current costs and summarizing current problems. This was contentious in itself since everyone was very defensive, but eventually we had a high-level picture of the current situation that was more or less agreed by everyone relevant. This work also reinforced our desire to obtain actual information about the current situation and helped strengthen our case to include a lot of time for this activity in the plan.

We also researched two areas: what was the expectation of outsourcing a fragmented and poorly run service in terms of a getting to a 'reasonable' level of service at what overall cost, and what should we build into the business case for investment in new technologies?

Our normal expectations of outsourcing are that better service can be achieved at a lower price. The skills and focus of the outsourcer can provide better service, and the economies of scale enable this to happen at a lower price. We expected a 20 percent saving to be achieved easily, over the first year or two of service delivery. This gave us the first points on our graph (Figure 4.1).

First steps in business case analysis

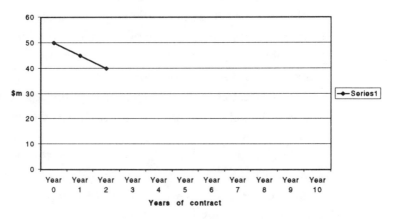

Figure 4.1

We then had to construct a model of would happen after the savings were achieved. Would the service run along at the same level for the remainder of the contract? To answer this question, we had to make sure that we understood the purpose of outsourcing in this instance. It was to help the business thrive. A minimal investment curve would therefore be unlikely to help this happen. Technology is moving fast and there are many (possibly as yet unforeseen) ways in which the business model will change. For example, e-commerce and the use of the Internet changed rapidly in importance over the life of the project. So we had to extrapolate a rising investment curve based on research into what was the usual growth in expenditure on IT. This figure was around an 8 percent increase year on year.

This enabled us to extrapolate a number of investment curves, two of which are included on the graph in Figure 4.2.

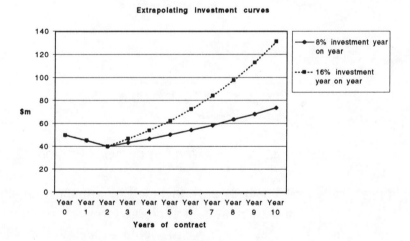

Figure 4.2 *Extrapolating investment curves*

This was not the business case as yet but a cost model that had some fairly alarming figures in it. To justify the outsourcing we had to develop the base case – what would be happening in terms of cost if nothing were done. But there were no plans for future investment, it just happened piecemeal. Looking at what had occurred previously, we found that IT costs increased in this company by 10 percent per year or more. So we overlaid this on our graph, shown in Figure 4.3.

This then provided the first crude financial justification for the exercise. Of course, this became both the basis of the business case and the target that the project team had to achieve in order to be seen to be successful.

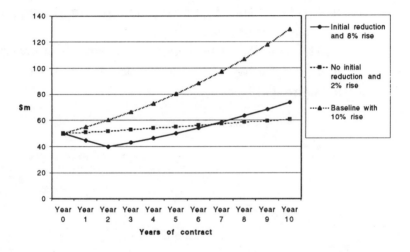

Figure 4.3 *Outline of the business justification*

The first business case included this financial justification and unquantified exploration of the problems and the solutions that we would expect the service provider to provide. These included better helpdesk services, configuration management so that consistency in versions of hardware and software was achieved within the two years and establishment of a corporate e-mail system.

The first business case also included an initial analysis of risks and the first risk register, which was maintained throughout the project.

Clearly, this first business case was a crude attempt to quantify the situation and decide whether there were grounds for proceeding with the exercise, and what assumptions had to be made for it to be worthwhile. As we progressed through the project, the business case was refined.

A business case can vary from a sketch or a line on one piece of paper to a detailed feasibility study running to 100 pages or more. Whatever the length of the document, its content matters more, in the sense that a good short poem is better than a mediocre long novel. The document needs to identify the existing problem or problems and list the actions that could be taken to resolve the difficulties. Naturally, the cost of each option over the life of a potential contract needs to be set down.

Essentially, the document presenting the business case is a comparison exercise, comparing the way things are done now in relation to the function in question with the way they could be done in the future if the outsourcing initiative goes ahead. It is absolutely necessary for the point of departure for the document to be a cost analysis of existing conditions (that is, how things are done at present). Unless this is so, it is difficult to see how the business case can make much progress.

The existing cost basis is the foundation and literally establishes a 'baseline' against which everything else is measured. Alternatively, it can be seen as a benchmark.

Formulating this baseline is rarely easy. Usually, employees and their managers don't really know what they have and own in terms of resources. It is very likely that there will be a fear of change, and even a reluctance to participate in drawing up the documents. Many people who work in medium-sized to large organizations do not feel that there is much connection between the overall performance of the organization and their own efforts, and are frequently much more interested in strengthening their own political position than helping the organization to be more successful. However difficult, establishing the baseline is nevertheless essential to the success of the outsourcing process.

Business case example (continued)

The first additional information that caused a major reworking of the business case was the actual information about the current situation. Collecting this information was an arduous process, and took place over a number of months. It provided a greater degree of confidence about the baseline, but was by no means the level of information suitable for a due diligence. In fact, the information was so difficult to collect and verify that despite the many meetings and verification visits we undertook, an extensive post-contract verification period was build into the transition.

This baseline was important for two reasons. First, it provided the current situation for the more advanced spreadsheets developed to calculate the NPV (net present value) and running costs of the deal. These spreadsheets formed the basic financial model of the deal across ten years.

Secondly, the service providers needed that information to be able to develop their own models of service improvements and prices so that we could compare the baseline with real, not hypothetical, offerings. Interestingly, all service providers bidding at this stage included the initial two-year cost reduction in their models. However, one alternative suggestion was to keep the profile flatter throughout the contract life, giving the service provider more leeway up-front but keeping the upward rise flatter later in the contract. This is illustrated in Figure 4.4.

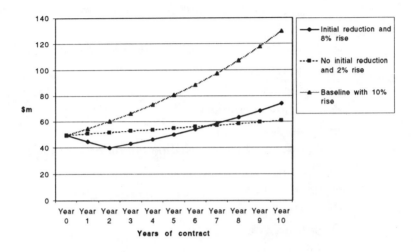

Figure 4.4 *Alternative pricing*

The process of developing the spreadsheet models continued throughout the negotiations with the preferred service provider and through the final approval of the project. These models examined every aspect of the costing and defined the NPV, which was the company's preferred method of judging business cases. Ultimately, there was a justification for outsourcing.

The business case provided the leverage for negotiating firmly with the service provider to get not just a good overall price, but the right profile of costs for the company's business position over the lifetime of the contract. It also convinced the board that the outsourcing should proceed.

The document outlining the business case needs to follow a logical and balanced structure. A document prepared in this way is likely to compel the writer to be as clear and logical as possible. In addition, the last thing busy people need is a long, complicated and rambling document; they want something to the point and pithy.

Ideally, the business case should contain the following key sections:

✢ Executive summary
✢ Strategic context
✢ Current provisions/existing conditions
✢ Options
✢ Benefits
✢ Costs
✢ Sensitivity analysis
✢ Risks
✢ The plan
✢ Recommendations

Executive summary

The executive summary could be argued to be the most important section in the business case. It gives the person backing the initiative (who will usually, though not invariably, be the person writing the business case document) the opportunity to be persuasive, rather like a barrister's opening address to the jury. Some busy executives may not read any other section. What they want is a simple, clear, logical précis of why the initiative is needed and what its benefits are, followed by a discussion of how the outsourcing arrangement will work, and what it will involve. This should be followed by an equally simple and compelling financial reason as to why they should endorse the sensible option that is being put forward.

The executive summary should, in essence, be a stand-alone document containing everything necessary to make a decision. Inevitably, decision makers will want to know more detail about some elements. Consequently, it is very helpful if the summary contains a good, user-friendly cross-reference system allowing quick and easy referral to the main document.

In our business case example, the executive summary was a specially written summary that captured the essence of the need to change with the benefits of the proposed outsourcing option.

Strategic context

This section sets the scene and provides the background to the strategic impulse behind the outsourcing initiative. It should present the organization's development in a global context if applicable, or in whatever other context is relevant.

The strategic context will also provide details of internal imperatives for a change of course being considered opportune. Generally, these imperatives will centre around cost efficiencies of some sort: economies of scale, standardization or – in the ultimate case – the company going broke if something positive or innovative is not done.

Finally, this section should make clear the scope of whatever the subject of the initiative is going to be. In some cases, this will be a very clear-cut, completely functional task with easily identifiable boundaries. However, life is not usually that simple, and if the subject is broad and complex, requiring a phased approach over a number of years, identifying the scope will be much more difficult. The entire argument presented in the strategic context must be clear and unwavering, without appearing dogmatic or to require special pleading.

The strategic context for our example company was that it was facing change. Markets had changed and customers were looking for a different kind of value. Moreover, its market had shrunk and was very unlikely ever to return to its former peak.

Current provisions/existing conditions

This section will inevitably require a great deal of time and effort to prepare. What is required is a description of the status quo in the organization, but that is never easy to define. In particular, what is required is not a statement of the duties that individual staff members complete during their working week, but rather an analysis of their overall contribution to the organization. Formulating that is much more difficult, and interviews with staff members may only be of limited usefulness in compiling the information.

Another problem is that it is necessary to put into the analysis the true cost of staff input to the function concerned, as well setting down the true financial value to the organization of their contribution. Quite apart from this, people – especially busy senior people – may be reluctant to devote time to helping with the analysis at all, especially if they know why the business case is being put together and are not supporters of the initiative.

Establishing the internal context is discussed in detail in Chapter 5.

For our example company, the implications of the strategic context were that it had to be more 'fleet of foot'. It had to change to address its customers' new needs, but also recognize that these needs would not last long before they would change again and yet again. Without change, the company would become more and more uncompetitive and, in an industry suffering a series of mergers and acquisitions, this would make it very vulnerable. Every part of the company had a role in responding to the need to change, but IT was unable to do so in its present form.

Options

The section on options details the high-level courses of action that the organization can pursue. Invariably, but not always, there are three principal options available:

✣ Maintain the current or existing arrangements – that is, do nothing.
✣ Improve the current or existing arrangements by use of in-house resources.
✣ Outsource – identify and select a supplier capable of delivering the required service.

Having identified the various options, a detailed assessment of them has to take place.

There were a range of ways in which the example company could have responded, ranging from minimal change to a more radical solution. Could it achieve better focus and change without assistance? It was thought unlikely that it had the expertise or infrastructure to effect change in IT itself. Everything was too thinly stretched.

Could the company change with external assistance and not need to outsource? This option was examined in detail and an alternative cost–benefit model developed. However, the long term was seen as too uncertain for the company to commit to large expenditure.

What would outsourcing bring both in terms of costs and long-term benefits? Would the company be able to sustain the relationship effectively?

Benefits

The purpose of this section is to set the parameters for appraising the options in terms of service quality benefits. It defines the criteria to be applied to each of the options, together with an estimate of the potential financial ramifications of the identified benefits.

The methodology involves ranking the benefit criteria on a scale of relative importance and then applying a weighting system. This produces a score for each of the options.

Typical examples of benefit criteria include reliability, service improvements, consistency, overhead and management effort. There are many more, some generic and others particularly relevant to the service being outsourced.

Direct costs will be analyzed in the next section, but each option will have an impact on a range of indirect costs, which can be summarized under three headings:

✤ Staff costs
✤ Costs associated with management time
✤ Cost differences through changes in business responsiveness.

Our example company had to consider what the various options cost and what benefits they might have. It could decide not to improve its IT and save money in the short term. What other benefits did outsourcing have to offer that made it attractive? Expertise in a fast-moving technology was key, as was a focus on delivering service unencumbered by internal politics. The discipline of having to deal with the service providers and using their professionalism to support the development of a more professional approach to IT internally were major selling points.

Costs

This section usually attracts the most interest and therefore it is pivotal to obtaining buy-in from the organization. However compelling the wider reasons for deciding to outsource, unless the case for so doing can be made fiscally, it is unlikely to be the course chosen by the decision makers. Generally, the board will not sign off the business case unless the financial director has given the all clear; and the FD in turn will have expect to have had the all clear from his or her subordinates (or subordinate FD in a group of companies).

The principal hurdle is getting the board to look beyond the short-term imperatives and focus on the long-term benefits. This is not as easy as it sounds, since in most cases in-year targets and current and year 1 and 2 budgets will have been agreed already. Therefore upfront additional costs in an outsourcing solution will not be well received.

The benchmark target in the cost section is accurately detailing the cost of the current/existing state, both now and over the contract life. The other options are modeled according to the relevant parameters. Some costs have to be estimated utilizing market-derived data. Again, these options are modeled over the contract life. All of this data should be displayed in a spreadsheet, together with a detailed breakdown of the assumptions used in formulating the financial models.

It is essential that every single option and variant of an option should be costed, since experience shows that the preferred solution is often a variation of the final recommendation in the business case.

A detailed analysis of all costs had to be undertaken to deliver the NPV (discounted cash flow) on which the financial case rested. In our example company there was a transfer of assets to the service provider, which results in an initial cash inflow as payment for the assets transferred. Other costs included:

+ Cost of the project itself, project team members and external assistance.
+ Overhead or 'lump' costs of service, e.g. on-site staff or basic service delivery.
+ Variable costs, which related to amount of service or volumes, e.g. helpdesk costs based on number of calls.
+ Specific or project costs that related to the day rates charged or priced on a one-off basis to reflect the need for a large-scale e-mail rollout.

Each cost was calculated based on the pricing of the service provider's proposal and a sensitivity analysis was undertaken, as described below.

Sensitivity analysis

As was mentioned above, a number of the assumptions made to model the costs and benefits of both the outsourcing and insourcing solutions are subject to estimation and therefore variability. The business case has to consider the key assumptions and provide a sensitivity analysis for them.

In reality, financial analysis is undertaken on a variety of 'what if?' scenarios. If, for instance, the outsourcing solution would halve contractor's costs, then an assumption could be made that this would increase profit before tax savings by £xm per year and after-tax cash flow savings by £ym per year. This process should be applied to all relevant financial variables, which will then result in best- and worst-case scenarios. The aim is generally to demonstrate that even under the most extreme of circumstances the outsourcing solution continues to be the most financially advantageous option.

Risks

A key component in any undertaking is identifying potential risks, their possible causes and subsequent means of management and ownership. Risks can be looked at in two ways: those affecting the project as a whole and, more importantly, those with an impact on the business case. Both should be included, but the focus of effort should be on those affecting the options identified in the business case.

Each risk should be scored against the likelihood of its occurrence as well as the severity of its impact. Areas could range from lack of interest on the part of suitable potential suppliers to the board's inability to make decisions at the appropriate time!

A risk analysis table is a cogent tool for reinforcing the senior management commitment that will be necessary to ensure success. A risk analysis table for our example company is in Figure 4.5.

Event	Prob	Sev	Potential causes of event	Likely impact	Ways to reduce probability of event	Whose role to reduce probability?
1 Loss of resources to complete project	B	1	a) Expert support leaves	a) Project fails	a) Buyer full commitment to expert support	a) Director
	D	2	b) Buyer project resources not available	b) Project fails	b) Buyer staff commitment to project	b) Director
2 Insufficient interest from appropriate suppliers to engage in a competitive pre-contract process	C	3	a) Supplier scepticism in buyer's good faith to proceed due to previous 'false starts'	a) Undue delay in appointing a supplier to commence negotiations, could include cancellation of project Excessive delay would delay the benefit of outsourcing for the buyer (including cash from the asset sale) and would render the figures in the business case outdated and obsolete	a) Provide assurances through initial letters of intent and/or a memorandum of understanding	a) Senior management assisted by the project team
3 Wrong supplier chosen	E	1	a) Poor selection process	a) Additional costs into contract a) End-user dissatisfaction a) Lack of business growth	a) Robust selection process	a) Project team, director and board
	B	1	b) Supplier imposed on project	b) Weak negotiation position b) Possible end-user dissatisfaction b) Higher costs	b) Robust internal communications to buyer board	b) Director
4 Senior management faces constraints in appointing a supplier to commence negotiations	A	1	a) Management is prevented by parent company and/or acquiring company from entering into significant contracts	a) Undue delay in appointing a supplier to commence negotiations, potentially could include cancellation of project	a) Obtain confirmation on position regarding management proceeding to contract	a) Senior management assisted by the project team
	B	1	b) Other strategic issues such as merger affect project	b) Cancellation of project	b) Robust business case must lead to firm board commitment	b) Director
5 Senior management of parent company do not accept the project's business case	C	1	a) Lack of rigorous data	a) Cancellation of project	a) Persistent business unit and project team verification of data Various data sources (e.g. business units, group finance)	a) Project team and management
			b) Lack of clarity of data provided by the market	b) Excessive delay would delay the benefit of outsourcing for the buyer (including cash from asset sale) and would render the business case outdated and obsolete	b) Reconfirm existing data, including (as a last resort) collection of new data Benchmarking exercise with cooperation of potential suppliers Reconfirm market data through additional benchmarking studies	b) Project team

Figure 4.5 *Risk analysis*

Recommendation

The business case must recommend the way forward. Everything should be guiding the reader towards this, the smallest element. There should never be more than one principal recommendation and it should be clear and unambiguous. It can have supporting statements, but they must be directly related to the main recommendation.

The plan

The business case should tell the whole story in a simple and logical manner. This story would not be complete without an indication of how the process will be conducted, what resources it will require and how long it is going to take to complete, i.e. when the organization will first see a tangible sign of the new service.

The most efficient way of displaying the process is on a Gantt chart, which breaks out all the necessary elements and activities of the process that must be undertaken. Most importantly, it should indicate when key internal approvals have to be obtained. This is an overt statement of confidence that if the decision to proceed down the recommended route is taken, there is a control and management system in place to deliver it.

For our example company, there were two plans at this stage: the transition plan for how the service provider was going to take over the management of the service and deliver the benefits, and the internal plan for what the company itself had to do, including:

✤ Completing the contract management structures and ensuring that all contract management staff were fully aware of their role.
✤ Continuing communications to staff and managers.
✤ Acting throughout the first intense monitoring period to ensure the smooth beginning of transition.
✤ Testing the reporting processes for real and acting on any need for changes.
✤ Reviewing progress.

Conclusion

In essence, the business case is one of the first tools in an outsourcing exercise and it continues to be used throughout to support good decision making. Even without a formal business case, there will be an informal case for or against outsourcing. It is therefore much better, in our experience, to make these issues, problems and benefits explicit.

5
Establishing the Context

*C*onsider two hypothetical organizations, each running their businesses more or less successfully. Are they likely to be doing this in the same way?

Clearly, the answer is no. Indeed, management consultants, business advisers and business schools all over the world are keen to explore the differences in how organizations operate. It is more than reasonable to suppose that no two organizations function in an identical fashion.

Now consider outsourcing and its implications for your organization. We have established that no other organization does its business in precisely the same way as yours. So when you decide on outsourcing, are you likely to be looking for exactly the same thing as your competitors are seeking? This is most unlikely.

What your organization is seeking from an outsourcing initiative is almost certain to differ from what your competitors are seeking, even if the competitor otherwise resembles you in many respects.

So how do you decide what exactly you are looking for? One obvious course of action is to draw up a list and try to set down everything you want to obtain from the outsourcing initiative by way of commercial and cultural benefits. Practical experience of this approach, however, tends to show that the list grows longer by the minute as you think of new ideas and of things (services, functions, tasks, activities, reports, actions) that you want the supplier to undertake. The more you think about it the more the list is likely to grow, until it is essentially a mere jumble of high-level services and lower-level tasks.

Experience shows that a more successful approach is likely to focus on the possible nature of the relationship with the outsourcing supplier. The relationship is only likely to work if the following are in position:

✛ a boundary defining the service provider's responsibilities, and the responsibilities of the organization that has appointed the service provider
✛ a way of measuring the success of the outsourcing initiative
✛ a definition of the nature of the relationship with the supplier.

Going back to the two hypothetical organizations, let us assume that one is a commodity business under a great deal of cost pressure, with a style that veers towards the autocratic, is hierarchical and is very focused on tangible cost savings. The other is more diversified and has a more complex requirement in terms of the purposes of the outsourcing initiative, which it regards as removing a distraction from management, improving investment in non-core areas of the business and helping to support growth.

These businesses may both identify outsourcing as helping to meet their objectives. However, the methodology of the outsourcing initiative could be radically different for each organization.

For the first organization, perhaps, outsourcing will involve a tough process of contract negotiation with the service provider. It will require the organization to be ultra-clear about measures of performance, defining these for as long as ten years at the outset of the contract, and expecting them to become increasingly challenging for the supplier to meet as the contract progresses. Very possibly, this organization has also accepted that it will be able to manage the contract in a tough way, keeping a focus on those performance measures and being confident that they are still relevant to their business success. That demands more than just a style, it needs skills and competencies within the organization that can manage contracts in this way.

But there is another model of outsourcing. Let us assume that this is closer to the model that the second organization is pursuing. In this model the organization recognizes that it may not be possible to define the outputs with precision over ten years and, even if it were, this would require an approach to managing the contract that is unacceptable to the corporate culture. People in the second organization may have no experience of such an approach and would be out of step with their colleagues and management if they did.

Setting growth and investment as targets for outsourcing may not always lend themselves to precise measurement. The problem is that there are often simply too many variables and dependencies. For example, how can growth be specifically attributed to only one part of an organization? Shouldn't all parts of the organization contribute to growth? How can each function's contribution be quantified? There may also be outputs from each function that are essential to the organization's growth, and these can be measured.

The approach that the second organization follows the methodology that we are advocating in this book. This begins by analyzing the current state of the organization.

The internal analysis and evaluation process

As we have seen, outsourcing is a management strategy by which an organization outsources major, non-core functions to specialized and efficient service providers. It is the strategic use of outside resources to perform activities traditionally handled by internal staff and resources. It is therefore extremely important to ensure that the internal situation is clearly identified before one can embark on a program of outsourcing. Indeed, previous experience has shown that those organizations that have carried out an in-depth internal analysis, research and evaluation are the most successful when outsourcing major, non-core functions.

As discussed in the previous chapter, the process of internal analysis and evaluation should be the first phase of the decision-making cycle. The cycle involves senior management in examining the need for outsourcing and developing a strategy to implement it. This phase is mostly internal and conducted at the highest level of the organization. Even if the idea for the initiative was put forward by someone working at a middle (or even junior) management level, the initiative is not going to get off the ground unless it receives senior management support – ideally enthusiastic support once the rationale for the initiative has been demonstrated to be viable. Ultimately, only senior executives have the power to implement the changes that are necessary for outsourcing to succeed.

Key issues that need to be taken into consideration as part of the internal analysis and evaluation process are outlined below.

Organizational goals in relation to outsourcing.

Outsourcing must be done carefully, systematically and with explicit business goals. Organizations that rush into outsourcing without fully understanding what they hope to gain may find themselves in a battle with a vendor who will supply services that make things worse rather than improving them. Outsourcing might be justifiable for a business unit with high costs that cannot be reduced or a lack of competence in specific areas. Organizational needs that might cause outsourcing to be considered include the ability to compete on a global basis or to obtain relief from financial pressures through immediate cost savings.

Organizations should make a positive choice to use outsourcing. Furthermore, they should understand the costs of a function and manage it effectively before evaluating its potential for outsourcing. They should consider (or reconsider) the overall merits of outsourcing at regular intervals (e.g. every three or four years). Revisiting the outsourcing issue may be particularly relevant under changing market conditions or when internal, industry or technology changes have occurred.

Functions to outsource

The nature of the core competence (the organization's ownership of the customer) and the functions of the business that are not core need to be identified. As we have argued consistently in *Inside Outsourcing*, an organization should outsource its non-core functions so that it can focus on its core competencies, because today's markets demand continually increased quality of product and services from every business.

Managers need to ensure that their outsourcing arrangement supplies two things. First, every segment of the internal value chain must add maximum value in the delivery to the end customer. Good outsourcing will ensure that this happens by securing specialist input to that area of the value chain. Second, outsourcing will free internal managers to focus not just on current core activities but, as the pace of change is also increasing in many areas, on identifying what will be the core activities in the future. A good co-sourcing relationship will ensure that the external service provider makes a contribution to identifying those future activities.

In order to identify the functions that should be outsourced, it is necessary to ask questions such as:

+ What is the nature of our customer franchise?
+ What are our core competencies?
+ Can we fix ourselves internally before we consider outsourcing?
+ What can an outside vendor do that we cannot?
+ What kind of relationship with a vendor is most appropriate?
+ What kind of contract will we need with vendors?
+ How will we deal with the people issues?

Long-term strategy

If a function that is already being carried out in-house is being outsourced, it is essential to remember that employee support and morale will be critical to the success of the initiative. Job retention should be a major feature of the outsourcing strategy; in some relationships, the new vendor hires employees. From the beginning, there should be honest and open communication with employees about how their needs will be met.

Research and baseline analysis

The second phase of the process of deciding whether outsourcing is the right way forward often has a more research-like feel to it, as people inside and outside the organization provide more detailed information and advice. This is the phase in which you learn about your own situation, your specific needs, and find out which qualified vendors will be best to meet those needs.

You need to research the needs within the organization, and learn from other organizations that have outsourced the same kind of function. Reference site visits will need to be set up with other organizations to find out what their experience has been. A team of people should be formed to ask the right questions and analyze the information gathered. Team members with expertise in the following areas may be useful:

+ legal
+ human resources
+ finance

✛ communications
✛ market research
✛ procurement
✛ any specific function to be outsourced.

In this phase the key objectives are to establish baselines and to specify the service levels required of vendors.

Baseline modeling/benchmarking

It is difficult to identify appropriate areas to benchmark without a clear understanding of what is driving the organization:

✛ its core values (what it really is, not what it wants to be)
✛ its core and support processes
✛ its competitive advantages and limitations.

Compare apples with apples

For a benchmark study to be useful, there must be some baseline for comparability of data. A organization should benchmark the performance or effectiveness of its operations against a comparable entity, or understand the differences of strategic position and operational requirements. Otherwise, it will be difficult to make valid comparisons to drive change. With abundant justification, it has often been said 'if it's not measured, it won't be done', and establishing baselines is certainly one example of this statement.

Avoid getting obsessed with numbers

Metrics can help measure performance and identify areas where change is required. Some organizations spend a great deal of time focusing on the numbers, data collection and analysis, but overlook the point of getting the data in the first place – to use the information to stimulate performance improvements. Furthermore, the number is less important than what it represents or what is behind it. For example, if an organization collects information about the total costs of supporting desktop IT to users, it needs to look beyond the statistics to understand the key issues. How does the in-scope support vary from the out-of-scope support? What is the effect of this on costs per user? Where can improvements be made and how can they be implemented?

The benchmarking process

How benchmarking is done will depend on such factors as an organization's objectives, resources and timeline. While several benchmarking methods exist, the process will generally entail the following steps.

Defining data requirements and scope of the study

During this phase, management will determine the type of data that needs to be collected, target outside sources of information, and plan the project. They will need to determine what type and how much information is needed to tell them what they want to know. Some organizations can collect far too much data and it is therefore important not to lose track of the objectives of the exercise.

Data collection

Sources of information may include analyst reports, published industry data, consultants, organizations that specialize in benchmarking, and customers.

Desktop IT

If we look at the example of outsourcing desktop IT, it can be very useful to carry out an IT survey. A survey would aim to establish baseline figures and to identify, for example, the total number of hardware units supported. Carrying out an IT survey in this way is an ideal means of counting and analyzing what hardware, software, servers, applications etc. the organization supports. Though extremely useful in establishing a baseline, it can be a very difficult process at desktop level, where purchase and installations are decentralized. Year 2000 compliance programs made many organizations draw up an accurate inventory of their desktop IT, but auditing the desktop should not be a one-off activity.

In an organization of any size, the inventory is bound to be out of date within a couple of weeks (in larger organizations, it is bound to be out of date within a couple of days!) and seriously inaccurate inside a year. This means there is a need for an ongoing management procedure that will keep track of what IT infrastructure exists and where it is located. An accurate audit of systems, headcount and costs is not an optional extra, it is detrimental to the success of determining the current situation.

Keeping up to date is not the only benefit of a desktop audit. Other potential benefits include:

✛ The discovery of equipment that the helpdesk did not know about. This means that the helpdesk can then gear up to support that equipment.

✢ The discovery of equipment that was not covered by any maintenance agreements or warranties, or equipment that is listed on maintenance contracts but no longer exists. Either way, there are opportunities to improve service or to reduce costs.

Data analysis

Again, in interpreting the data it is important not to get lost in the magnitude of available data. Once analyzed and verified, the data should be used as a 'zero base' document to assist in future comparisons. Often the data is a key element in the business case for outsourcing, as it details the current situation and signifies areas where change is required.

Benchmark on an ongoing basis

Once the process of benchmarking is understood and the initial benchmarking study has been completed, the process should continue. The organization, business groups, business units and sites need periodically to benchmark their internal figures and performance in order to make continuous improvements. To maximize the benefits, benchmarking should be an integral part of managing the operations, rather than a separate and distinct activity. It should be incorporated into the strategic and operating planning cycles to understand where the organization needs to change.

6
Planning

Once you have decided that outsourcing is to be part of your business strategy, it is critical that your approach to the arrangement is structured and systematic in order to gain the benefits you are seeking.

Shreeveport has worked on over 150 outsourcing exercises ranging from the tiny (and certainly unsuitable for outsourcing) through middle-sized (sometimes unsuitable) to the large and very large. One lesson has stood head and shoulders above all others: it is essential to have a well-defined methodology or approach if you are to succeed.

Preparation of a plan of action is essential. The relationship between the plan and the reality can be compared with the relationship between the substance of an iceberg and the comparatively small part that is visible above the surface of the water: what you see above the water represents about one seventh of the real mass. Planning is much the same. The inputs into planning are big and the outputs may look small in comparison; but all effort put into making the plan realistic and likely to work pays dividends in multiples of the original effort, as well as

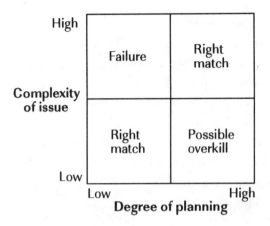

Figure 6.1 *How detailed should your plan be?*

in terms of smooth running when the plan is executed.

Figure 6.1 illustrates the relationship between the complexity of a potential outsourcing initiative and the degree of planning required.

The nature of the plan

At the very minimum, the plan needs to set out what must be done, by when and by whom, and with what resource(s). It also needs to focus on the *how*, not the *what*.

Consider the difference between contracting and outsourcing. In contracting the customer owns the process, and asks the supplier to provide specific tasks. In outsourcing, however, the entire business process is turned over to the supplier, and the supplier owns the process. What does that mean to you, the customer? It means that the question you should be asking is not 'how' the process will be done, but 'what' the results will be.

A plan can be defined as a set of instructions:

- to someone
- to carry out a certain thing
- in a prescribed manner
- within a given timescale
- with a finite set of resources.

It defines a set of actions but it is not action. Until someone does the actions outlined in the plan, nothing will happen.

The plan will:

- have measurable objectives
- answer questions that interested parties should be asking
- build in contingencies
- identify risks and set out actions for avoiding or minimizing consequences.

In addition, a plan gives:

- a degree of confidence
- a framework within which to work
- confidence that everything has been thought through
- evidence of consideration
- a means of communication of the contents to others in a logical, consistent and robust manner, facilitating discussion and debate.

Having said this, the method or approach is not going to be the same for every set of circumstances. The first key issue is to define the objectives, as described below.

Preparing the plan

In Shreeveport's experience, 12 key stages must be addressed in preparing an outsourcing plan. This is a simplified version of the Structured Procurement Approach that we use in our consulting assignments.

- ✢ Clarifying objectives/requirements.
- ✢ Planning the process.
- ✢ In parallel, determining potential suppliers and their level of interest and establishing a dialogue.
- ✢ Managing your managers/key stakeholders.
- ✢ Communicating with staff involved, with other staff and with those outside the business.
- ✢ Shortlisting suppliers and providing them with your information/requirements.
- ✢ Evaluating their responses and continuing dialogue.
- ✢ Getting your senior managers signed up to what you want to do.
- ✢ Identifying and training your contract management team.
- ✢ Negotiating the contract and agreeing service level agreements.
- ✢ Transition, determined by the earlier stages of the process.
- ✢ Managing the contract in the way agreed with the supplier at the negotiation stage.

These stages are not necessarily in the order in they occur. Objectives must come first for the exercise to be sensible. However, we have come into outsourcing exercises after the selection of the preferred supplier where the objectives have not been thoroughly defined. For example, the operations director has identified the need to get better internal structures and free up staff time, so has outsourced distribution.

But beyond the internal benefit of not having the hassle, there are no objectives for the new distribution company. Less cost? Better timekeeping and reliability? Who knows! The operations director is no longer being bothered by his staff, but in a few months' time anything could happen.

It is also an unfortunate fact of life that not all organizations have an 'enlightened' view of communicating with their staff. While we would plan to be communicating from the word go, if only to explain who we are and why we are around, some organizations believe that telling people nothing means they know nothing. Of course, the reverse is true – telling people nothing means that they 'know' lots and lots, but this usually consists of rumor and suspicion, misinformation and inaccuracies.

Getting your senior managers signed up is not a late entry into the activity list – it must be done early and continuously. Senior managers have a lot on their agendas and they need to have their interest and attention stimulated as the project progresses.

Setting objectives

No sensible person would embark on an exercise that will cost a great deal of money, take a large amount of management and staff time, and have a significant impact on the business without having clear objectives – or would they?

Picture the scene at a first or second board meeting after the outsourcing supplier has taken over. The chief executive reaches the agenda item on outsourcing, and looks around for comments on its success. The financial director clears her throat and says that the savings she expected are not clearly materializing. The commercial director says he can't understand this: 'We wrote a good contract, which was watertight and really tough on the supplier.' The customer service director says that he thought service was supposed to improve, but it hasn't, and many customers are complaining. The HR director says that staff who transferred to the supplier have been leaving for new jobs and maybe that's why service is poor. The CEO thumps the table and yells: 'What was it supposed to achieve?' A hush falls. Somehow, nobody appears to know the answer.

This type of scenario is all too common. Shreeveport's research shows that the majority of organizations do not define the objectives for outsourcing and often feel afterwards that it is not a complete success – but our research also shows that 74 percent would nevertheless outsource again.

Start out by defining what you want to achieve, and how you will know that you have met your objectives. Research will often help in realistic goal setting at this stage, and much of this may have been done when you were preparing the business case. If you are seeking cost cutting, what is the industry standard for savings from outsourcing that function or service? A poorly run area of your business could produce significant savings of at least 20 percent and probably more. A better-run area should yield cost savings of about 10 percent.

This may also lead you into thinking about what you could do in advance of outsourcing to get an even better deal. Outsourcing a mess will possibly result in a mess and, worse, gives all the easy wins to the supplier. Fixing the mess may mean that you can take these easy pickings yourself and then use the supplier's expertise and size to give you even greater benefits. It can be a good idea to link these objectives to your own business performance. Perhaps the supplier could help your staff be more productive, perhaps they could help you to meet your business objectives.

Supplying food

Take the supply of foodstuffs to supermarket shelves. The key factor is to ensure that the customer can get the product when they need it. Miss the early-morning rush for sandwiches and you miss the market for that day and possibly affect the market on the next day. You may understand this, but does the logistics company that supplies you?

A major logistics company supplies temperature-controlled foodstuffs to a large food retailer. The logistics company's challenge and its success are measured by the fact that the food is on the shelves when the customer needs it. In the City of London, this means from 7am onwards. And the logistics company has the responsibility of getting it there on time to meet each day's peak hours. Catch that window and both companies are successful.

So think through what would assist you in achieving your business goals and what the supplier can do to help this happen. Then you can set the objectives for the outsourcing arrangement.

These objectives need to define not just what you want out of the exercise as a whole (i.e. what you expect to happen after five or even ten years of outsourcing), but also something about the process and the way that the outsourcing is being approached. For example, it may be necessary for your organization to achieve key stages of the outsourcing process (e.g. contract signing) before the end of the financial year, or that some sale of assets or transfer of staff must be completed to a key milestone in order for you or your managers to meet their business target. Therefore you need to plan carefully how you are going to go through the process to meet both the long-term objectives and the intermediate needs of key stakeholders.

Planning the process

The list of 12 stages described above can form the high-level plan for the activities that need to take place, but detailed tasks, outputs and dependencies need to be built up that reflect the features of your starting point in your organization.

Key planning lessons that Shreeveport has learned include the following:

✢ The amount of communication required for senior managers, middle managers and staff is often underestimated. Outsourcing can often be a people-intensive process.
✢ Contract negotiation can take far longer than you estimate – a rough rule of thumb for a difficult contract is to make a really generous estimate and multiply that by six. To minimize the time involved make sure that you keep lawyers out of the negotiations for as long as possible, and when they are involved remember to manage them tightly – a bit like keeping a firm grip on a damp eel!

Part of establishing what the plan will be must also be to determine what the relationship with the supplier is likely to be, as discussed in Chapter 3. The process for contracting out or old-fashioned outsourcing will involve you in a great deal of up-front work in writing the specification. The supplier(s) will formally respond to that, which will be evaluated by the team, who will select the preferred way forward and negotiate finer points of the contact before concluding the deal. As part of this approach, the supplier will need to perform a 'due diligence' exercise on your organization to satisfy themselves of the basic facts. In this approach once the contract is signed, you will have your baseline service level agreements (SLAs) and any deviation from them will go through formal contract change control.

However, if you are seeking a more collaborative and participative relationship with your supplier, you need to provide a statement of objectives that will form the basis of your contract and agreements and then allow the supplier to undertake a post-contract verification (PCV) exercise, while it is running the service. At the end of the PCV, you formally agree the initial SLA against which service improvements can be measured. In this way, both you and the supplier could conclude the contract negotiations more quickly and may be able to achieve transfer of assets or people according to a shorter timescale.

Nevertheless, it is essential that the rapidity of the process does not lead to sacrificing any thoroughness or care in handling the human resources involved in outsourcing or in getting the contract right to protect both participants. What it does mean is that the approach is not going to be driven by data but by common objectives. And this kind of process will demand an honesty and openness on the part of both your organization and the supplier (subject to strict commercial confidentiality).

Determining potential suppliers

Determining potential suppliers may involve examining the 'liquidity' in the supplier market for your particular services.

General Insurance Standards Council

For example, in the UK financial services market a new regulatory body, the General Insurance Standards Council, is being set up as a 'virtual organization', i.e. its activities will be done on an outsourced basis. These tasks are fairly unusual and there may be an issue about ensuring that there are suppliers able to provide them.

You will need to ask the following questions:

✤ Who are the players, what are their strengths and weaknesses?
✤ Do we need to 'create' liquidity by negotiating with potential suppliers where this represents a new venture?
✤ Has the supplier done something similar before?
✤ Can we see reference sites?
✤ Can we provide an outline brief of the outputs and outcomes required so that potential suppliers can respond to this?

Managing your managers/key stakeholders

This stage is about telling the key players what is happening and taking their objections on board. It needs to be carried out in three dimensions: emotional, political and rational (Figure 6.2).

You have to counter people's fears about the consequences of the initiative for the organization, demonstrate the cost/benefit issues and address their worries in relation to how it will affect them personally. Communication is the essence of the whole matter: communication of the business case both within the organization and to outsiders who will be significantly affected by the outsourcing initiative.

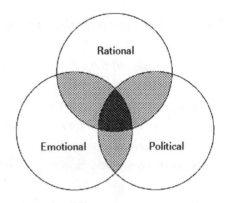

Figure 6.2 *The three dimensions of persuasion*

Shortlisting suppliers

Reaching a suitable shortlist of potential suppliers
and supplying them with a statement of requirement
should be planned to include all the following areas
of activity:

✤ Developing the statement of requirement (SoR)
   and supporting documentation.
✤ Qualifying the information in the SoR and determining cost and service baselines for measuring
   success.
✤ Collecting and collating other useful background
   information so that potential suppliers can respond
   fully.
✤ Making initial and if necessary subsequent market
   contacts to find suitable potential suppliers (this
   may not be necessary with large projects).
✤ Developing an evaluation method and criteria
   before much supplier contact is made to ensure a
   reasonably objective assessment of potential suppliers. A formal evaluation group may need to be
   established and trained in the evaluation (depending on whether this level of formality is required).

✛ Organizing meetings with suppliers, reference site visits and suppliers' presentations.

Each of these activities comprises a range of sub-activities and tasks with many interdependencies. If very senior management or the board will be involved iₙ supplier contact meetings, scheduling can become a major problem.

It will therefore be critical to plan sufficient elapsed time to complete these activities, but emphasize that board involvement must also be within critical deadlines (not an easy task!). Nevertheless, board-level involvement should be encouraged as much as possible. If board members 'own' the deal it is more likely to be seen as successful.

Evaluating suppliers' responses

Planning supplier evaluation raises a number of issues that must be addressed at the outset of the project:

✛ The evaluation framework needs to be devised so that the criteria that will drive the evaluation are reflected in the briefs and requirement documents that the potential suppliers receive.
✛ What level of management can evaluate the responses? How many are on the shortlist, so how much work will be involved?
✛ How is the decision-making process going to work? Does the evaluation panel report to the board?
✛ How is the process to be described to the potential suppliers? Will they be given the chance of feedback?

The actual process of selecting the supplier is described in Chapter 7.

Getting your senior managers signed up

As well as planning to communicate with your organization as a whole, managing senior management is important. Plan in time to support and retain their enthusiasm for the outsourcing process, and identify the key milestones for their approval, such as:

+ furnishing an initial shortlist of suppliers
+ agreement to the scope of the exercise and later to the statement of requirement
+ meeting potential suppliers and visiting reference sites
+ selecting a preferred supplier
+ agreeing to the contract.

Remember that preparing reports and presentations to the board can be time consuming, as quality cannot be compromised.

Identifying and training your contract management team

The focus in developing the plan for the outsourcing process tends to be the period up to contract signature. Running the contract will be a far longer process and must deliver the benefits sought. When evaluating suppliers, the quality and training of their contract management personnel will be part of your evaluation of their bid. But it is easy to forget that you must also have contract management staff, and that they must not be transferred to the outsourcer. It has sometimes happened that at the end of the contract negotiation managers look round an empty room and ask: 'Who's going to run this contract on our side, then?' Don't let this happen to you.

Negotiating the contract and agreeing SLAs

Negotiating the contract is an area where estimating time can be notoriously difficult. The process of ensuring that key contractual points are exposed as early as possible must be planned – but clearly there may be unforeseen 'showstoppers' that will need to be addressed.

One approach to negotiating contracts is known as the 'locked room' method. This is where all parties are shut into a room to get all contract details agreed, and are not allowed out until agreement is reached. It may be an approach that suits your organization. However, the subtext is that if the parties who are in the room cannot agree, the deal is off. This is obviously an undesirable outcome. It can be avoided by making sure a deal is 'do-able' by good preparation, and by ensuring that the real decision makers are those who are locked in the room.

If you want your organization's decision makers away from the business for as little time as possible and you want them to be very well prepared, it becomes evident that one way to achieve this is to delegate as much of the negotiation as possible, using key decision makers only at the end to finalize the contract. Either approach will work, provided that you plan it effectively.

There is more on the contract in Chapter 8.

Service level agreements

You need to plan the development of a baseline service level agreement (SLA) in parallel with negotiating the contract, as the risks that the contract assigns will be dependent to some extent on the SLAs. The SLAs will be schedules (annexures) to the contract and therefore must be available when the contract is signed.

SLAs usually consist of a number of processes or components:

+ Daily data-collection processes – collect information such as response times, transaction volumes, jobs missing their deadlines etc.
+ Exception control – report measurements that have exceeded thresholds.
+ Daily or weekly reporting – produce online reports to track service levels.

Not only do SLAs provide the basis for measuring service provision, they are also a powerful management and communications tool for both the service provider and the customer, to the mutual benefit of both.

However, in planning the development and agreement of the SLA, you must be aware of the definition of service. As stated before, it is important to define requirements in terms of outputs. The provision of these outputs form the basis of the service, and the levels of service can be established by defining acceptable service and how it will be measured. Some organizations will find it relatively easy to define outputs and measures and agree acceptable or improved service levels. Many organizations, in our experience, do not.

One example of an organization that set service levels, not just for Year 1 but throughout the contract, is a major steel manufacturer when it outsourced its IT provision to EDS. The culture of this organization was such that managers could define their service requirements. If your organization is

likely to find this difficult, then plan in several itera-
tions of service level definition, and plenty of valida-
tion with front-line or shopfloor managers.

Transition

It is difficult to plan transition – the change after the
start of the contract from the current service to the
agreed outsourced service – in any detail at the outset of the outsourcing exercise. It will be defined by
potential suppliers (because you ask them to in your
statement of requirements) and negotiated during
contract and SLA negotiation.

Unfortunately, there is often a general belief that
outsourcing will make a change from day one of the
contract. To some extent outsourcing will make a
change – people and assets may be transferred, new
managers will be in place and responsibilities shifted.
But it is clearly unrealistic to imagine that an outsourcer can achieve change and deliver improved
service levels within 24 hours, as the process of
change takes time (if it was that easy you would have
done it already).

How much time and what will be achieved need to
be agreed, and will depend on:

+ where you are now – with a well-documented,
  managed function or in a mess with little knowledge of current performance
+ where you want to get and why – improvements in
  service; reductions in cost; or room to focus on core
  business. These are different objectives that could
  be met in different timescales
+ whether there are any key milestones or deadlines
  to be met.

Suppliers tend to like longer transitions than client organizations often seek. Fairly obviously, the longer they have, the lower the risk of not achieving the goals. But even the initial plan should be able to identify the critical deadline, e.g. staff transfer before the end of the financial year; cost reduction in the last quarter; or productivity improvements within six months. This kind of goal is probably the best you can do to plan transition until supplier negotiation has taken place.

An example of a transition plan is given in Figure 6.3.

Project Outsource – 05 May (D Day) to 12 July (Contract sign)

ID	Task name	Apr 01	May 01	Jun 01	Jul 01	Aug 01	Sep 01	Oct 01
29	Plan due diligence at corporate level	27/04 ▓▓ 12/05						
30	Plan due diligence at group level	27/04 ▓▓ 12/05						
31	Plan due diligence at site level	27/04 ▓▓ 12/05						
26	Identify site LOs		06/05					
27	Brief site personnel		06/05 06/05					
28	Due diligence undertaken		06/05 ▓▓▓▓▓▓ 09/07					
32	Due diligence completed				12/07			
33	Contract signed				12/07			

Figure 6.3 *Sample transition plan*

Managing the contract

There are even fewer possibilities for planning this stage effectively until after the contract is signed. The process of contract management will be developed as part of identifying and training contract management staff. A plan of contract management must be developed at that time, and can only be thought about at this stage. It is, however, worth bearing in mind that contract management will be necessary and cannot be left to chance.

Conclusion

Without a thorough plan, you cannot hope to succeed with a major and complex project such as outsourcing. It is therefore vital to ensure that you allow sufficient time and resources for this aspect of your outsourcing exercise.

7
Selecting the Service Provider

To select a supplier you need to define what you want the supplier to do; be aware of how you are going to assess the response you get to your approach; and be clear how you are going to manage the relationship with them. In parallel with developing your end of the deal, you need to be sure that there are organizations that are both interested and capable of undertaking your business and with whom you want to form a strategic relationship.

As can be seen from the 12 key stages identified as part of planning the process, the essential complexity of outsourcing rests in Stages 3 to 10, which are about selecting the service provider, although many organizations tend to regard this as constituting the entire preparatory phase of the outsourcing activity. These stages may not be the longest in terms of elapsed time, but they may be the most intellectually demanding and challenging in terms of gaining and maintaining management buy-in to the outsourcing deal.

Selection of the service provider begins after the initial goals are defined and the planning is under way. It ends when the contract is signed and the process of changing from the current regime to the supplier – transition – begins.

Two models of selecting the service provider

Figure 7.1 shows what might be described as the ideal methodology for selecting a service provider.

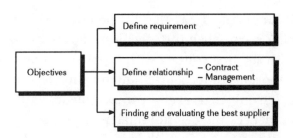

Figure 7.1 *Realistic outsourcing activity timing*

The approach adopted by many organizations often turns out to be more linear (Figure 7.2).

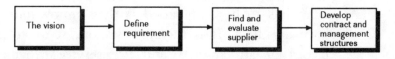

Figure 7.2 *Linear contracting approach*

Unfortunately, the linear approach leaves little opportunity to be sure you have a workable relationship with the supplier, and too often the contract and the customer management processes were supplied by the selected supplier so need to be tested in your organization.

Our experience shows that three things must be pursued in parallel:

✛ developing the specification of service, with quantified baseline, growth plans and trends
✛ outlining the contract management structures and
beginning to identify candidates to fill contract
management roles
✛ establishing the evaluation process and framework,
and devising evaluation criteria.

The specification of service

It is not true to say that the process of selecting a supplier starts when the specification is written. It begins
with the first contact with suppliers. In fact, it is very
important to recognize (and for suppliers to take it as
a lesson) that every contact made with suppliers
influences the decision-making process.

It may be that high-level contacts and impressive
clothes are seen as a reason for choosing a service
provider. It may also be that such factors have a negative influence on the project team, who view themselves as being sidelined by senior managers who go
on the golf days and enjoy the wining and dining. But
what has to be understood is that impressions do
have an effect. It is therefore important to keep a
record of all contacts and use service providers'
actions as a sensible way to reach an understanding
of the relationship they are seeking. Do they pursue
issues up the corporate tree until someone decides in
their favor? Or do they talk at a senior level and work
together at a day-to-day level to ensure they get it
right?

That said, the formal process of assessment of
capability (as opposed to suitability) only begins
with the specification of service is drawn up. This is
the 'brief' that the service provider will need to

follow, and ideally enhance according to its own expertise and experience. An example contents list for a statement of service requirements is shown in Figure 7.3.

Developing the service specification should include the following steps.

Specifying the outcomes or outputs that your organization requires

We have explained elsewhere in *Inside Outsourcing* the difficulty of getting current staff to 'buy in' to outsourcing. Those providing the service are often exactly the wrong people to ask to specify the requirements that the service provider must meet. This is because:

+ they may be opposed to outsourcing and may seek to scupper the whole exercise
+ their core skills may be far removed from those needed to write a specification
+ they may have no idea of your organization's requirements but be thoroughly knowledgeable about the current position. These may be two different things, and current providers may find it difficult to see that.

British Forces

For example, a female consultant at Shreeveport was assisting with an outsourcing exercise for health services for British Forces in Germany and the then current providers were helping to write the specification. Asked to provide an example of the specification for review, the male doctors chose a topic called genito-urinary medicine (GUM) as the review subject. Their specification

CONTENTS

1 INTRODUCTION
   1.1 Context
   1.2 Purpose of program manual
   1.3 Structure of the statement of service requirements

2 BACKGROUND AND OBJECTIVES
   2.1 Introduction
   2.2 Outline of the procurement
   2.3 Background to outsourcing
   2.4 Buyer's objectives of outsourcing

3 CURRENT SITUATION
   3.1 Introduction
   3.2 Quantitative analysis
   3.3 Qualitative analysis
   3.4 Current provision of IT support

4 STATEMENT OF REQUIREMENTS
   4.1 Introduction
   4.2 Summary of requirements
   4.3 Services excluded from the scope
   4.4 Services in scope
   4.5 Service item status

5 SERVICE LEVEL REQUIREMENTS
   5.1 Introduction
   5.2 SLA structure
   5.3 Current service measures/levels
   5.4 Service measurement system
   5.5 Future service levels

6 PHASED IMPLEMENTATION, TRANSITION PLANNING AND BEYOND
   6.1 Introduction
   6.2 Phased rollout
   6.3 Transition planning
   6.4 Post-contract verification
   6.5 Multiple business units located on a single site
   6.6 Human resource and communications issues
   6.7 Requirements

7 DUE DILIGENCE
   7.1 Introduction
   7.2 Aim of due diligence

8 COMMUNICATIONS AND HR
   8.1 Introduction
   8.2 TUPE – Transfer of Undertakings (Protection of Employment)
   8.3 TUPE requirement and communications

9 CONTRACTUAL MATTERS
   9.1 Relationship background
   9.2 General contract objectives
   9.3 Principles governing the relationships
   9.4 Contract monitoring
   9.5 The supplier's financial health
   9.6 Quality
   9.7 Staff training
   9.8 Allocation of the supplier's key employees to the contract
   9.9 The supplier's non-key employeees
   9.10 Procurement and engagement of subcontractors
   9.11 Invoicing
   9.12 Payment terms
   9.13 Managing other providers on behalf of the buyer
   9.14 Change control
   9.15 Changes to workload volumes
   9.16 Issue management and resolution
   9.17 Service continuity
   9.18 Disaster recovery
   9.19 Contingency planning
   9.20 Transition plan
   9.21 Insurance cover and liability management

Figure 7.3 *Example of service specification contents*

included an explanation of the detailed methods for tracing sexually transmitted disease contacts and the presumption that all patients were male and all contacts were female.

Two changes were needed and forcefully pointed out by our consultant – first, that tracing of contacts was the critical outcome, and detailing current processes could hinder the achievement of that by directing tracers wrongly; second, making things gender specific meant that the service provider would have no contractual obligation to trace contacts of the other sex.

Writing the specification requires a knowledge of the full extent of what is produced to ensure that nothing is missed in the specification so some kind of joint team is often needed, using external advisers and coupled with training in the principles of specification production.

There are some key things to remember when producing an output-based specification:

✦ List the outcomes you want, i.e. what must happen. Then list the outputs, i.e. what must be produced to make this happen. Check the interrelationship between these things carefully – will output *X* really help *Y* happen, and will it always help *Y* happen? Don't allow yourself to be carried away by one scenario and so forget that there are different situations that may change cause and effect. Do these outcomes really help meet the outsourcing objectives (which were set earlier – remember?).

✦ Don't make the outcomes more grandiose than the service provider can deliver, or assist in delivering. If the service provider could make your business performance better, maybe it should just take it over. What can the service provider contribute given the service that it will be providing?

✛ Within the boundaries you have set to the outsourcing, does the service provider have everything needed to deliver the outputs? This is particularly true of asset transfers. For example, the UK Ministry of Defence has, in the past, retained some assets essential for delivering the service. This breaks the service provider's supply chain and means that if performance falls there are many opportunities for the service provider to say: 'It was your bit that failed – I'm within my performance limits.'

We did some work for MOD Bovington – an artillery training school – to review a specification for outsourcing the training. The service provider would have use of many assets, but not the transport for trainees to the training ground (a fairly short drive). These assets were being kept because the buses were fairly new and the specification said that the MOD would supply the transport. But this gave the service provider no responsibility for getting the trainees to the training if the buses broke down or in other circumstances. And in practice, where there were problems with transport (the drivers might be called on for other duties) the trainees missed their day's training.

This was changed in the specification so that the service provider had to deliver the outcome of X days' training to the trainees (there were other performance measures related to levels of pass marks and length of time for trainees to pass the course). As this could only be done at the training ground, they had to get everyone there to meet the outcome.

✛ Make sure you get to the real issue.

We once read a specification about tending the grounds of a magnificent Queen Anne building. There was an output about the state of the lawns. However, it specified the length of grass that was acceptable. This was not even a range of lengths – the grass had to be two inches long. Surely the point was to keep the grass trimmed, which was part of the larger point about keeping the grounds neat. There are times when keeping grass very short is detrimental to its survival. This specification was overprescriptive even in its outputs.

✤ Check the time part of the outcome – is this from day 1 of the new contract or later on? The new service provider will not be able to get to the steady state of service delivery on day 1 if the current situation is far from the ideal.

This brings us to the need to understand where you are now.

Baselining where you are now

This may seem somewhat pointless to the staff who may have to:

✤ measure or count things for the first time, even down to assets to be transferred
✤ work out the time they spend doing things
✤ actually measure performance, if only for a few months before the service provider starts.

However, if you don't have a baseline you will never know whether you're achieving benefits or not.

With services that have been provided in-house it is often the case that few costs are specifically allocated, as measuring service costs and inputs, e.g. staff time or other resources, is simply not done.

Performance may only be measured by adherence to budget, and with a few major projects visible to the organization. In some cases, this lack of detailed accounting is not unreasonable – why should you spend time counting resources, allocating costs or measuring performance when the organization as a whole is not (formally) interested in the outputs? It is only when queries like 'Is it value for money?' or 'What do other organizations spend on similar services?' begin to be asked that measuring is seen to matter. And, of course, both these questions need to be asked and answered as part of the outsourcing exercise.

In practice, it may be impossible to summon up the resources or enthusiasm for measuring something that is in any case going to change radically. At this stage in the outsourcing process it may be better to spend your time and energy on creating the right relationship and really seeing what each service provider has to offer than on introspectively examining your own company. You must know something to set the size of the area to be outsourced. But collecting a large amount of detail is not necessary.

You may decide to get the right service provider and then allow that company to do the counting and set the baseline. You can check or sample its work to assure yourself of its veracity. And you have a relationship with the service provider, don't you? This will be worth more to it than trying to rip you off at the beginning (or you haven't done your job properly). The service provider will need to do a due diligence or a post-contract verification (PCV) in any case, so you may as well share that and agree on the baseline at that time.

Defining what sort of relationship you want with the service provider

If you don't get the relationship right, everything will be hard work. Once you have set the objectives, you inevitably begin to think about how you will work with the service provider. You may find that people in your organization want to gain the upper hand and control a service provider with a rod of iron. Others may be looking for a 'partner'. As we have described in Chapter 4, the external relationship will be defined to some extent by the culture of the organization. And getting it right will inform every aspect of outsourcing – not just the specification and the baseline as already described, but the way you manage service provider contacts, the evaluation process and contract management structure that are appropriate, and the contract and performance levels you put in place.

It is useful to start to think about the relationship as you begin to produce the specification and develop the baseline. This is your side of the relationship and you need to define it – if you like, it is your dowry and you must use it to get the best spouse! But then you must think about the characteristics you are seeking – you should look not just for characteristics you like but also for whether they have the coverage you need: geographic spread, technical ability and good processes. You should also look for a past history (are there many broken hearts behind the groom?) with good site references and valid experience. But first you must be sure that you can define what you want before going down the aisle!

A good tip is to think about the end: the contract and what it will contain. If many people in your organization want to 'punish' the service provider for misdemeanors in performance, you may need a hard adversarial relationship or to work on changing the culture to one where you both thrive.

The first area in defining the relationship is the type of agreements and contracts that will form its legal basis. These specify:

✤ the agreement reached – who does what
✤ who has which responsibilities
✤ termination provisions, both at the end of the contract and for special reasons during the contract
✤ service levels
✤ service credits or penalties for non-performance
✤ how the contract may change and who will do what if requirements change
✤ pricing mechanisms, including 'caps' on changes.

There may be aspects of the service which are volume sensitive but which, realistically, you cannot afford to fund indefinitely.

Rolls-Royce

Rolls-Royce aero-engines division outsourced its IT provision to EDS. Part of the outsourcing arrangements included the IT helpdesk, which EDS took over and improved by using established helpdesk management and systems. Calls to the helpdesk increased greatly. Charges on use of the helpdesk were based on call volumes. Even with charges levied in bands, so that they are not infinitely variable according to each call, EDS's charges for running the helpdesk increased.

In another similar situation you might recognize the extra work that the calls generate, but that does not mean that you can afford to pay for them. What can you do? The answer lies in analyzing both the past and the alternatives. What did people do before the helpdesk worked so well? Did they ask each other for help or get help some other way? Or maybe they struggled, made mistakes and contributed to poor business performance. If so, you should be glad to pay for a helpdesk that improves individual performance because the whole business will benefit.

Alternatively, analysis of who and why people are calling may help determine the underlying causes of the calls. Maybe the supplier needs to be given a cap for helpdesk calls and the remit (and reward) for training – if they do more training the number of calls may be within financially viable bounds, and your organization will have a more competent workforce – a genuine win/win relationship.

Defining the relationship also involves deciding on the contract management structures and processes that you need to put in place to ensure that you get the best from the contract you've signed.

The structures, processes and people who will form the interface with the supplier must also be identified and tested early in the outsourcing process.

Devising the evaluation approach is often overlooked early in the process. It is assumed that the evaluation criteria can be developed once the specification has been issued and your organization is waiting for suppliers' responses. This is hopelessly too late. How can anyone devise a specification unless the key aspects of the requirements are agreed? These key aspects must therefore be what you will look for in supplier responses. It therefore makes sense to put these things into the evaluation model as you identify them in the specification.

Similarly, as you devise the specification you should think through how you will manage the interface with the supplier. This will give you a first cut of the contract management structures – only a first cut because the supplier may have completely different proposals that demand a different response from you.

While clearly the ability to do the job is important, having a good cultural fit and the right attitude between the two parties are recognized as essential components of a good relationship. And the definition of that relationship – as a 'partner' who is involved in ensuring business success or as a subcontractor with a job to do – is part of your requirement. Don't let the supplier drive you on this.

Listing potential candidates

An essential next step once you have defined the service specification is to generate a list of potential candidates. Don't ask the purchasing or procurement department to do this: ask your marketing department to help by identifying possible candidates in the widest possible sphere. Gather as much information as possible, analyze that information and ask your corporate planning or strategic planning department to analyze the real opportunities these companies could present.

Shortlist questionnaire

Develop a basic questionnaire for suppliers to enable you to cull this 'long list' of potential candidates down to a 'shortlist'. The questionnaire should address the following key areas:

✢ Is the candidate a publicly quoted organization, private limited organization, consortium or partnership? If it is a consortium, list all members.

✣ Request the last three years' audited accounts.

✣ What is the annual turnover? What is the annual turnover specific to the service you are interested in outsourcing?

✣ Has the candidate ever been in administration or liquidation?

✣ Has the candidate ever been prosecuted for violations of health and safety at work legislation?

✣ Ask for copies of the candidate's policies in the following areas:
  - health and safety
  - security
  - quality management
  - equal opportunities
  - industrial relations
  - environmental initiatives.

✣ List membership of any trade associations.

✣ Is the candidate ISO9000 accredited or equivalent? If so, ask to see a copy of the certificate.

✣ Does the organization have professional liability insurance and for what amount?

✣ How many staff are employed in the area in which you are interested?

✣ What percentage of staff turnover does the candidate experience on an annual basis?

✣ Request a brief synopsis of work undertaken for current clients.

✣ Have any of the candidate's contracts been terminated at clients' request and if so when and why?

Go through the responses diligently and then arrange a visit. Don't ask the candidates to come to you, preferably go to their locations and look at their existing operations.

This is not a task that you can delegate to middle management. It requires senior managers who have the widest possible vision of how a supplier could contribute to your success.

When undertaking the visit it is essential that you check:

+ What are the candidate's core competencies, track record, client and sector knowledge?
+ What are its systems and process capabilities? In particular, understand how its strengths match your weaknesses.
+ What are its aspirations and aims? Is your operation going to be central to its objectives?
+ Will your organization be a large or small client for the candidate? What sort of commitment can you expect?
+ Last but not least, understand the candidate's culture. Cultural fit is essential to success. Choosing the right partner is like choosing a spouse – it can be disastrous and expensive when it goes wrong!

Evaluating suppliers

The process of selecting a supplier should be regarded as funneling potential candidates through a series of progressively finer sieves towards final selection.

To achieve this, evaluation must be a continuous process throughout the contact with prospective suppliers. This mirrors the way the human mind starts processing information the moment we meet people, deciding, it is said, within six seconds whether we like the person or not. Because every meeting, telephone call, note, memo and visit contributes to the subjective view of the potential suppliers, we must also look at some way of developing an objective view in parallel.

This objective view is important for a number of reasons. Outsourcing is a commercial decision, not a personal one. The exercise will only be considered successful if the business objective is met. The evaluation process is about producing objective information against which you can measure whether the objective is likely to be met. This is the basis of the business case for outsourcing.

The evaluation process should therefore include identifying a number of criteria that reflect the business objectives, for example:

✢ The technical ability of the service provider to deliver.
✢ The depth of experience in the particular field of delivery.

When we were outsourcing the delivery of healthcare to UK service personnel and their dependants, for example, we had to look for some proxy for experience as this was a unique service provision contract – no one had done it before.

✢ The culture of the organization.

In outsourcing the healthcare provision we looked for cultural fit – military organizations tend to have a different culture to social services, for example, and the service provider had to recognize that and be able to work within it.

✢ Understanding of your organization's requirement and the situation. You will have told the would-be service provider a great deal about your organization and its 'world'.

We undertook an exercise looking at the opportunities for outsourcing and risk sharing in another military training organization with regard to initial soldier training. A key characteristic that the organization looked for in service providers was an understanding of the 'military ethos', i.e. the motivation of soldiers.

✛ Special characteristics that you know you need.
✛ A separate set of criteria for financial evaluation to ensure that you receive value for money.

The evaluation process must also alert you to any risks of outsourcing and what can be done to manage them effectively.

Insolvency Service

When we were examining the benefits proposed by suppliers wishing to undertake the work of the Insolvency Service, which services insolvents and bankrupts, no supplier could overcome a lack of specialist expertise in its proposals. This risk was evaluated and measures for its management proposed. However, this was not enough to convince senior management to proceed.

Finally, the evaluation process must be communicated to managers and staff in your organization. That there is a structured evaluation process that will lead to the choice of the 'best' supplier is a positive message to broadcast – a supplier for services affecting everyone's future won't be chosen on the 'old boy' network or because of wining and dining, but rather because there is a sound reason for it.

To be effective the evaluation must:

✛ be based on the objectives of the outsourcing

✛ allow for all kinds of contacts with suppliers to be recorded and considered for evaluation, in a way that is not too arduous.

The outcome of the contact should also be noted. At formal visits to reference sites there should be standard evaluation questionnaires and reports for each visiting team member to complete. These should focus on different areas, e.g. human resource expertise and record with transferred staff, or contract management approach. Outcomes can be scored, each score weighed in accordance with business priorities. The scores for, say, visits, assessment of formal proposals or initial contract discussions can all be further weighted and accumulated to give suppliers a ranking.

Where the process can be less formal and therefore more in keeping with organizational culture and strategies, evaluation may be less about scoring and more about a general positive or negative impression. Senior management's evaluation of meetings may be as scant as 'general impression – favorable/unfavorable'.

Request for proposals

In parallel with developing the evaluation framework and processes, a formal request for proposals (RFP) should be developed and distributed to the suppliers shortlisted from the initial questionnaire.

The RFP must contain:

✛ The specification you have been writing.
✛ Background – this is particularly important if there is little (or no) historical data that indicates trends in the usage or performance of the service up to the

present. It is also important to give the supplier the opportunity of coming up with innovative ideas to help you meet your business goals. Indeed, the degree of innovation may be part of the evaluation criteria.

✤ Instructions for bidders – telling them how to respond.

British Forces Germany

When we were evaluating responses for suppliers in outsourcing healthcare provision to British Forces Germany, one element that we were actively seeking was an idea of how to break away from the current service and the current thinking about service provision, in a way that would meet not just the needs of troops and dependants overseas in the mid-1990s (when we undertook the exercise) but also in the future, given that we could not predict whether the post-Cold War situation would continue as it was or change radically.

It is part of Shreeveport's philosophy that giving suppliers as much information as possible will help in the evaluation process. You will be able to tell whether, as a bidding team or as an organization, the potential suppliers can process the information you give them and add some value to your organization's business as a result – or do they merely repeat what you told them or, a serious danger sign, ignore it and carry on in their own not-so-sweet way?

In addition to providing the specification of requirements and the background, you should tell suppliers how you want them to respond to the RFP. This serves two purposes.

First, as part of a comparative evaluation it is useful to have everything in a similar format, prices reflecting the same units and so on. This will make evaluation much more straightforward. Conversely, it is amazing how different responses to the same question can look when you ask more than one supplier. Don't underestimate how irritating it will be to your senior management to have different things to compare or how much work it will take for you to rework all the numbers so that every bid is on the same basis. This is the suppliers' job, so make them do it!

Second, it will give you some indication of how easy the supplier will be to work with. If it does not produce its bid in the format requested, or its prices are structured in a unique way, it is right to ask whether it is really seeking to work with you or whether the relationship will always involve the supplier doing what it wants and your having to like it or lump it. Of course, a supplier may respond with an innovative way of answering your questions, but this should be in addition to helping make your life easier by providing easily comparable responses.

Supplier contact

Throughout the outsourcing exercise suppliers will – and should – be keen to meet your outsourcing team and managers in your organization. There is a view that the whole outsourcing process should be made as difficult as possible for the supplier – if they can stand it, we'll award the contract to them. This may be appropriate if you want an adversarial relationship with the supplier after the award of the contract as well as before. Make no mistake, how you run the relationship during the exercise will determine how the suppliers think you will run it once the outsourcing has happened.

If outsourcing is to be used as a strategic tool, then an adversarial approach probably won't give you what you want. There needs to be a more constructive, not destructive, relationship. The objective is that the whole – you and the outsourcer – add up to more than the sum of the parts, i.e. more than you can achieve separately.

Therefore, during the period when you are selecting a supplier, begin the relationship as an open, constructive one. Provide information, see suppliers and visit them, facilitate supplier meetings with your senior managers if they are willing. The relationship need not be uncontrolled just because it is open. Ask the suppliers to channel contacts and requests for information through key individuals. Ask them to provide you with a diary of their contacts with your organization. Get cross if they do not respect your 'rules of engagement', because it makes your life harder not easier.

In this way you can gauge whether the supplier will fit with your style for a long-term constructive relationship.

The contract management team

The supplier's contract and service delivery managers need to be part of the process so that you and your contract manager can meet them and get to know them.

It is important that you get to meet the manager(s) who will be responsible for the provision of the service, not just the supplier's sales team. You may find that you get on very well with the sales team but that the nominated service delivery manager (SDM) is unacceptable. If this is the case ask for another SDM to be appointed, and make sure that you have the contractual right to demand that key personnel are changed if they do not fit (but expect some compromise and do not exercise this right unreasonably).

We did an exercise with a major retailer. Although the sales team was great, one man was a really difficult character. He argued at length over trivial points and would not make even a minor compromise during negotiations. It turned out that he was designated as our SDM!

Involving your contract manager is also important, as he or she must be comfortable with the process and the supplier selected if the outsourcing is to be successful. If you have not identified your contract management manager or team, then do so early, as this will lead to a better result.

Throughout the outsourcing exercise, you will need to manage your managers, the board or whoever has given the mandate to pursue outsourcing. It is part of good project management practice to have an overarching steering group that at least approves the stages and outputs of the project. In an outsourcing exercise, you will need to do all of this and more.

Remember that outsourcing is a strategic tool – the benefits to your business should and could be considerable, but the potential for knock-on change is also considerable. Possibly greater benefits could be gained from using the outsourced service in a different way. Maybe you need to change the business substantially to achieve this. Would your management sign up for reengineering?

Benefits Agency

The first well-run outsourcing contract may pave the way for more. We saw this in the Department of Social Security Benefits Agency, where initial outsourcing revealed so much promise that innovative benefit-based (no pun intended) relationships were developed to help manage a leviathan of an organization employing 90,000 or so people in England, Scotland, Wales and Northern Ireland.

Developing the SLA

The service level agreement (SLA) forms the bridge between the specification of requirements and the contract. It must contain both the requirements and the measurements of service. It is helpful to separate requirement and measurement so it is absolutely clear what must be achieved and how you will know if it is achieved. The SLA can be developed from the service specification, but the measures will determine how challenging the contract will be for the supplier. Levels of service will determine price and if the measures are very demanding price will be higher than if they are not.

For example, a 24-hour telephone support center means that the supplier has to staff the center on a shift basis, with increases in training and management levels over, say, a 10-hour telephone support center. As you proceed with detailed contract negotiations, the price of this service may be an issue and you may want to explore whether, as your organization currently manages with an 8-hour sporadic support desk, 24-hour support is really necessary or would merely be nice to have. You can judge this according to your knowledge of the organization, the value to it of the service levels you are seeking, the impact on price of changing the requirements, and the scope for other trade-offs as part of the negotiating process.

Communication

Throughout the process of selecting the service provider, it is important to remember that information about the outsourcing decision must continue to be communicated to all affected staff.

You could of course decide to conduct the exercise in secret.

Steel manufacturing

A major steel manufacturer in the US outsourced its IT to EDS and undertook all meetings and negotiations off-site, informing staff only after the deal was done (when the news would have broken in any case).

However, it can be difficult to keep things this quiet. Rumors will abound and create a great deal of uncertainty and fear in everyone's mind. It is better to be open and issue communications, phrased positively, that indicate that outsourcing is being considered and that there are benefits for staff as well as for the organization.

In our experience it is fear and uncertainty that generate staff turnover, not outsourcing. When there is no announcement about what is happening, rumors usually include far worse projects than outsourcing, including mass redundancy and closure of the department. Avoid this by communicating what it is reasonable to impart, and continuing to communicate during the exercise and the transition to the new supplier (and thereafter, to manage expectations of service and deliver good news of measurable improvements!).

8
Legal Aspects of Outsourcing

*A*ny practical experience of outsourcing shows that it creates a number of significant potential legal complexities that will require the input of experienced professionals.

Out of necessity this chapter is written in fairly formal language. We use the terms 'purchaser' and 'supplier' here to denote, respectively, the organization entering into the outsourcing arrangement and the service provider.

There are two main reasons for legal complexities being virtually inevitable in outsourcing arrangements. First, outsourcing involves two entities entering into an extremely intimate commercial relationship, rather than a one-off transaction. Such a close relationship means that there is a greater chance for human folly and for things to go wrong, which in itself is a recipe for legal complications.

Second, legal complexities are inherently likely to arise from the fact that the relationship will often entail close day-to-day contact and access to each other's confidential information. The supplier or service provider will also be providing goods and services which, although not core to the purchaser's business, are still very important in allowing the purchaser and its staff to perform their tasks. Any disruptions to the provision of the necessary goods and services, such as IT and facilities management, could potentially have a catastrophic impact on the purchaser's business.

Despite their becoming 'partners' of sorts (with the precise nature of the partnership depending on the nature and style of the outsourcing arrangement), the purchaser and the supplier are still distinct entities, with different environmental pressures, different strategies, different commercial interests and, ultimately, different owners. Where things go wrong, each side will ultimately have to act in its own interests at the expense of 'the partnership'.

As a result, it is essential for the purchaser and the supplier to allocate rights, obligations, powers, risks and rewards properly to allow the relationship to be conducted smoothly, and to allow possible disputes to be resolved as quickly and painlessly as possible.

Conceptually it is convenient to split the legal issues into two categories:

✛ the contract and related documents to get the relationship started
✛ other miscellaneous legal issues that arise over the course of the relationship.

The memorandum of understanding

The contracting process in an outsourcing scenario, particularly in larger arrangements, often needs to be broken into two stages: a memorandum of understanding (here abbreviated to MoU), and only later the full contract.

In some larger organizations MoUs are a regular part of everyday procurement, while in some other organizations even experienced senior procurement managers have not heard of the term.

An MoU is a shorter type of agreement that is a statement of intent between the parties to give each other comfort of their good faith in proceeding to a due diligence and contract negotiations. Suppliers particularly need this comfort, particularly if they are required to commit significant financial and human resources to a due diligence and contract negotiation process.

An MoU is generally not legally binding like a contract; the obligation is moral rather than legal. However, the parties should not sign an MoU lightly. The MoU signing often coincides with an announcement to the staff, the public generally and, if the deal is big enough, the media and the investment community. Accordingly, there is the potential for embarrassment if one side has to pull out after this announcement.

The MoU is a fairly brief document, probably anything between four and twenty pages. It sets out in non-legal, general language the broad objectives of the parties. The most basic objective is to proceed to negotiate a contract for a particular duration. The MoU would also express very broadly some of the principles to be embodied in the contract, particularly in the difficult areas that are potential causes of disagreement during negotiations.

One of the advantages of having an MoU is it allows the parties to explore their intentions and share their broad attitudes to some of the potentially more difficult parts of the deal. It is a way of the parties determining early on in the process whether they are near to concluding a deal or whether they are poles apart. It is a lot cheaper and cleaner if they can discover this early, rather than find out later during contract negotiations, after significant resources have been committed.

The contract

A good contract should set out in clear and precise terms and in ordinary language the scope of the work to which it applies and define clearly the roles, responsibilities, liabilities and expectations of the parties governed by the contract. If there is a dispute or any party fails to perform as the other expects, then procedures and remedies should be available and be clearly stated. The contract should enable the customer to achieve value for money while allowing the supplier to make a reasonable profit. Reasonable targets and performance measures should be laid down, as should the payment terms and conditions.

However, the contract should not be unnecessarily arduous, as any supplier who feels tied to an over-rigorous contract may well be tempted to cover the risk financially, possibly by reducing support costs or increasing the margin on the goods or services provided. A contract should not be viewed as a stick with which to beat the other party. There is, above all, a need for balance in the contractual relationship.

At the simplest level, the customer needs the required goods and/or services to be of the right quality and to be delivered on time and at a reasonable price. Nowadays everybody is seeking 'value for money' rather than simply the best or cheapest price. The customer needs a clear contact point with the supplier at the appropriate level of authority to be able to commit to the smooth delivery of the goods and services. Customers also don't want surprises to emerge and would prefer any issues to be raised early, with any identified problem accompanied by one or more potential solutions where possible. The route for resolving difficulties and, as a last resort, a clear disputes procedure should be laid down. Customers want reasonable payment terms with monies to be paid after delivery and on acceptance of the goods and/or services. Customers would naturally like to keep their options open and have suppliers who are keen to succeed for the good of the customer, not just for their own profit motive. It is obviously very important for customers to have suppliers who understand their business and needs.

On the other hand, the supplier has to make a profit and be paid on time, on reasonable payment terms without large retentions. There must be a clear definition of the goods and services being provided, with reasonable timeframes for delivery, and of the responsibilities of the supplier, stating precisely who the buyer is. The supplier must be able to understand, manage and therefore meet the customer's expectations and have access to people who can help them understand more fully what is needed rather than what has been specified. There must be a clear escalation route for resolving difficulties and as a last resort a clear disputes procedure.

Any supplier would want to increase their chances of winning further business and creating opportunities for future sales. All suppliers would prefer no surprises to emerge and for issues to be raised early, with a minimal exposure to risk and incurring minimal overhead in supplying the goods or services. Constructive feedback at all levels on suppliers' performance would be useful, as would an open and honest approach from the customer. Fundamentally, suppliers need to be accorded respect for their industry and business acumen.

Outsourcing contracts are usually thick, detailed documents. They are often subliminally viewed as symbols of conflict, pessimism and mistrust, which is frequently at odds with the spirit of goodwill and optimism that exists between purchasers and suppliers when the relationship is still fresh and generally untested. Contracts may even be seen as an evil simply devised to line lawyers' pockets.

There are four main reasons that drawing up a comprehensive, thorough and precise written contract is important:

✤ The contract is an important risk management tool. It foresees different situations, issues and problems that may arise over its duration. It should foresee events that may seem unlikely, and should 'assume the worst', just as fire extinguishers and lifeboats are there in case the unthinkable happens. When problems and disputes arise resulting from that inevitable visitor, human folly, a well-written, comprehensive contract should serve as a consultation document to allow the parties to resolve the problem quickly and inexpensively. Where a contract is vague or incomplete, there is a much greater chance of disputes ending up in court, leading to expensive litigation costs.

✤ The contract negotiation process, and the task of formally expressing the intentions of both parties in clear, precise, written language, are good ways to help both the purchaser and the supplier formally crystallize their understanding of their expectations of the relationship. Both processes force all parties to understand exactly what they must do, when and how, and what they can expect from the other side. The formulation of clear expectations is very important to help budgetary and other planning.

✛ A written contract is often helpful as a communication tool. If an outsourcing arrangement is to last a significant duration, say five or ten years, that arrangement must be able to continue even if the individuals who negotiated the contract leave their respective organizations. The intentions of the purchaser and the supplier should not simply reside inside the heads of the negotiators. A contract serves as a written, historical record to communicate the intentions of both parties at the time.

✛ A good contract can be used by the service provider as a working document.

What should go into the contract?

The contract will be a legally binding document, but a detailed knowledge of the law as such is not the most important consideration for drawing up a workable and satisfactory one. The greatest skill lies in structuring the deal in a way to meet the objectives of both sides, and being able to express the intention of the parties in clear language.

The skill in structuring the deal lies mostly in understanding the organizational behavior aspects – how different groups of people will work together to meet the respective interests of the purchaser and the supplier, and how they will deal with the various issues and problems that will arise over the contract's duration. Understanding the financial implications of the arrangement is also an important skill.

For outsourcing arrangements that are expected to last for three, five or even ten years, it should be remembered that, as a general rule, one-sided contracts do not last. If the contract is heavily weighted against the supplier, there is a significant risk that the other side will lack enthusiasm and commitment. Service levels may drop, and the supplier may try to win back some value by imposing hidden costs on the purchaser.

The general structure of the contract

The contract will generally be physically structured in two parts:

✛ The terms and conditions – these will be clauses covering the general aspects of the relationship between the purchaser and the supplier. They cover the rights, powers and obligations between them generally, without being specific to any particular part of the service.

✛ A number of annexures (sometimes called appendices or schedules) – discrete documents covering the small-print detail on certain self-contained topics. These annexures are legally binding. The types to be included will depend on the nature of the service and the circumstances of the contract. However, they will generally include documents such as service level agreements, details of the transition plans, and the details of the sale and any leaseback of any assets. Also, if it is necessary for certain numbers of the supplier's staff to be permanently located on the purchaser's sites (which is common), there is likely to be an annexure covering a license to occupy that office space.

Managing poor performance

The parties must address how to manage situations where the supplier fails to meet various performance targets set for it under the contract. The contract must be able to deal with a range of different kinds of failures. Any remedy must take into account the nature and severity of the failure, the level of blame that each of the parties bears for the failure, the speed and effectiveness of the rectification, and the extent to which a failure is a 'first-time offense' or a common occurrence.

Termination of the contract is an extremely drastic solution, and should be restricted to the most catastrophic event, which is likely to happen very rarely. The vast majority of failures by the supplier will be fairly minor, and unlikely to create too much damage to the purchaser. These failures will only cause some temporary nuisance or inconvenience to the purchaser's staff, and might include the breakdown of air conditioning for a few hours in the middle of summer, or the late delivery of a PC. It is still important for the contract to address these minor failures: individually they may appear minor, but if they accumulate into regular occurrences, the reputation of the supplier among the purchaser's staff might decline, which may not reflect well on the contract managers who appointed that company!

There is no particular standard right or wrong way to manage poor performance. One way may be for the contract to introduce a points system for breaches. Each service specified would contain a range of points to take into account the severity of the failure, the importance of the breach, and the speed and effectiveness of the supplier's efforts to rectify the problem. Points would be accumulated for all instances of failing to meet service standards, and the purchaser would receive service credits off its monthly fees otherwise payable. Accordingly, if the supplier causes too many problems, this will be reflected in lower remuneration for its services.

Accommodating unforeseeable changes

Depending on the type of service and the duration of the contract, both parties can expect the contract to change over time. The contract will effectively be a 'living document', and the purchaser and the supplier may virtually be in a continual state of negotiation with each other. Changes to the contract may be made for a variety of reasons. They may be required to add or remove services originally incorporated, to adjust prices, or to clarify any ambiguities.

Contracts will tend to require more constant, on-going negotiations and changes if they are of a reasonably long duration, and where what is being outsourced are not standard, commodity-type services.

Contracts for more commodity-type services, such as cleaning, will generally require less renegotiation and change because the service is unlikely to change much over the contract's duration. IT and 'soft services' contracts are likely to be at the opposite end of this spectrum; given the rapidly changing nature of these types of services, it would be difficult to anticipate all aspects of the contract from the beginning. The contract would be changed as and when the technology and the purchaser's needs become apparent later in the life of the contract.

Although it would be impossible to anticipate the changes to be made at the time the contract is originally negotiated, it is essential that from the beginning the contract covers the process for changing its terms, often referred to as 'change control'.

A clear process is there to protect both parties, but more so the purchaser. Without an adequate change control process the purchaser would run the risk of entering any renegotiations with a relatively weak bargaining position, and therefore at a distinct disadvantage. The reason is that once the supplier is installed and is expensive to remove, it can potentially behave like a monopolist with the purchaser. The supplier could virtually employ a 'take it or leave it' approach, and the purchaser does not have the same ultimate sanction of 'showing the supplier the door' as it does when the contract is first negotiated.

There is no particular boilerplate solution for a change control process. It should be designed to meet the specific circumstances of the purchaser and supplier. It must take into account matters such as the level of trust between them, and the extent to which the bargaining positions of the two are likely to be unequal when changes to the contract are being negotiated.

In the main, the change control process is likely to cover a number of areas, particularly the following. The first is the process to escalate problems to the respective senior managements if the representatives from the two sides cannot agree during renegotiations.

Another area to be covered is the process for ensuring that the side with the stronger bargaining position in renegotiations (usually the supplier) does not abuse its position against the side with the weaker position (usually the purchaser). This process will often involve using reference points such as benchmarks to ensure that the side with the stronger bargaining position is not taking the other side for a ride, and that its offering matches the best currently offered by the market at the time. Alternatively, the supplier may agree to open its books to the purchaser to show the supplier's costs and margins, in order to satisfy the purchaser that the prices being quoted are reasonable.

Another area concerns the physical procedural protocols for commencing and conducting negotiations. The contract would describe how one side can initiate renegotiations, and how the other side must respond.

Termination of the contract

Another difficult area in structuring a contract is the clause describing the situations where either party may unilaterally end the contract before the end of the agreed duration.

This section often causes significant problems, particularly for purchasers who have not built up much experience in outsourcing. Around the purchaser's organization senior managers will be asking: 'Are we committed to this for ever? Can we get out of it if it doesn't work?' The fear of an irrevocable commitment to the unknown is a natural one, and must be addressed in the contract.

The contract should provide a comprehensive description of the events that would allow one side to terminate it unilaterally. It should also provide a description of the process required to trigger and complete a termination. This process would also cover the supplier's exit process, which is likely to include the handover of assets back to the purchaser and the transfer back of staff.

Limitation of liability

The limitation of liability question is important and needs to be addressed in the contract, although it can often be a difficult point in negotiations.

Under the contract law of England and Wales (and also of other Anglo-Saxon, common-law countries such as the US and Australia), when two parties are in contract and one of them breaches causing the other damage, the perpetrator is generally liable in damages to the victim for all consequential damage that is not too remote from the breach. This includes economic loss, such as lost profits. However, the parties can contractually agree to exclude or cap the liability of one party to the other.

While outsourced services are generally not core to the purchaser's business, they are still often services critical to the smooth continuity of that business. For example, if IT is outsourced and the system is down, the entire production of the purchaser and its staff can come to a halt. This may sometimes cause the purchaser significant economic loss, particularly if the disruption happens at a crucial time, such as the purchaser's failure to meet a contract deadline for one of its customers. Technically, the supplier could be liable to compensate the purchaser if it lost profits from a contract due to the supplier's being unable to deliver. If it happens on a crucial deadline date, the losses can be enormous.

On the face of it, in an outsourcing scenario it would appear that the purchaser should be reluctant to exclude or cap liability. It might well ask: 'Why not let the damage fall with the cause?'

However, the risk of liability for such damages effectively represents a cost to the supplier. This cost may often be directly reflected in professional indemnity insurance premiums. These costs are effectively passed on to the purchaser through the prices in the contact. Accordingly, both the purchaser and the supplier would have to think carefully about the economic consequences of imposing uncapped liability on the supplier.

Financial viability

One risk for the purchaser lies in the ongoing financial viability of the supplier. If the supplier's financial problems were sufficiently severe to cause it to cease trading, the purchaser might be left high and dry with no one to provide the required services. Sometimes this can happen with little apparent warning. Any unforeseen disruption could have serious consequences for the purchaser, particularly in areas such as payroll where the purchaser's employees depend on being paid on time.

The likelihood of some of the major international outsourcing providers going out of business may seem very remote, and the chances of this happening would statistically be very low. In some cases, the providers have brand names known across the world and are almost like small nations. However, bear the following points in mind.

Many of the providers are service companies, often owning very little in the way of hard, tangible assets. All they really have are cash and receivables under their contracts, which themselves are only as good as the customer that they are serving. The provider's cashflow would be at severe risk on the termination of a couple of bigger contracts, perhaps through poor performance, the customer going out of business, or the natural expiry of the contract.

Many providers have extremely short – even alarmingly short – histories. In the world of IT outsourcing, for example, many of the best-known international providers have existed for fewer than 20 years, some for fewer than 10. The financial future of a relatively new large organization such as Microsoft may seem assured, but how can a company be certain that some other relative newcomer will turn out to be a suitable and reliable business partner?

Even the seemingly impregnable empires of Rome and Britain came to an end, so there is no reason to think that the IBMs of the world will necessarily last forever. Large companies do occasionally go bust, sometimes with little warning to their customers and to the world around them. There is no good reason to think that outsourcing providers are any more immune than other industries.

The contract in itself will not prevent the supplier's financial problems from occurring. Even the best contract cannot prevent the ravages of human error, the economy, or whatever else may cause a supplier financial problems.

However, the contract can help establish a process to allow the purchaser to foresee whether financial problems are on the horizon. Any prior knowledge of such problems would allow the purchaser to take the necessary steps to minimize the effects of disruption. This may entail putting an alternative provider in place.

The process will largely entail the supplier providing the purchaser with certain relevant information, such as financial reports, business plans, details of any lawsuits, and details of the termination of the supplier's other large contracts. On a regular basis, the purchaser would analyze the information provided to form a view on the supplier's financial health.

It should be recognized that even the best process will not be infallible. Like unaided flight and mind reading, predicting the future is a skill that humans have coveted but never convincingly achieved since ancient times. The flawless prediction of the future financial health of a company is no less an elusive skill. However, at least some process of monitoring and analyzing the supplier's financial position will increase the chances of identifying potential problems on the horizon.

General sundry obligations

The contract should also cover certain sundry obligations between the parties. These may include confidentiality and security. Given that the purchaser and the supplier are likely to enter into an intimate relationship, they are likely to be privy to some very confidential information about each other. This confidential information may include the following:

❖ private details of the purchaser's staff: this would be particularly relevant where payroll is outsourced, where the supplier would have access to details of pay and other similar private matters
❖ information of a commercially sensitive nature, such as the purchaser's business strategy, and about development of new products
❖ information that would affect the purchaser's share price, such as that about a proposed acquisition by the purchaser
❖ information confidential to the supplier to which the purchaser may wish to have access: under the contract the purchaser may require the supplier to provide details of its financial position, business plans, strategy and any pending disputes and law-

suits with its other customers. Details of the supplier's costs and margins may also be passed on to
the purchaser if open book accounting is used.

The contract should at least require the parties to
keep each other's information confidential. The only
exceptions would be in relation to information
already in the public domain, or if it is required by
law to disclose that information, such as under oath
in a court of law. The contract should also go further
than just keeping information confidential. It should
ensure that each party passes on this obligation to its
staff, subcontractors and advisers, and takes responsibility for any breaches.

The contract should also require the parties to
keep information secure, whether held in paper or
electronic form.

Reporting and auditing

When outsourcing, the purchaser will effectively
divest itself of the capacity to closely monitor provision of the services involved. For example, the purchaser is unlikely to maintain asset registers, or
closely measure, say, how many lightbulbs were
replaced. The purchaser in particular will no longer
monitor satisfaction levels among its business unit
managers and users.

These tasks will be passed on to the supplier.
However, given that the purchaser is still accountable
for its own business, it retains an obligation to keep
track of its resources. Accordingly, the contract will
generally require the supplier to furnish the purchaser
with regular reports on a range of relevant matters,
such as service usage and user satisfaction. These
reports will be prepared on a self-assessment basis.

In an outsourcing scenario the purchaser is unlikely to have retained the resources to check the supplier's reports closely. However, to ensure that the purchaser has confidence in the reports on the service that the supplier provides, the contract should allow the purchaser a right to audit the supplier's record-keeping and reporting procedures. The purchaser would naturally be under no obligation to use that right of audit, and in practice should use it sparingly for cost reasons. However, the right should still be in the contract in case it is needed.

Invoicing and payment terms

For the supplier the most important part of the outsourcing arrangement is being paid. It has obvious cashflow considerations, and delays in being paid can seriously affect its financial position. Accordingly, there should be very clear provision in the contract on invoicing and payment terms and procedures.

The purchaser generally has two main considerations in this process. It would first wish to ensure that it is properly charged only for the goods and services that it has satisfactorily received. Second, it would wish to ensure a smooth, orderly process to keep its own invoice-handling costs to a minimum.

Ideally, the contract should prescribe a strict invoice format and frequency. It should also prescribe where the invoice should be sent, and the deadline of a day in a particular month or quarter. In theory, if the invoice deviates from these requirements without the purchaser's permission, the invoice would be technically invalid and the purchaser would not be liable to pay it. However, in practice, the supplier would ensure that its systems are set up automatically to comply with the agreed procedure.

The contract should then cover how the purchaser is to deal with valid invoices. It would set a period of time over which the purchaser is expected to investigate the invoice if it requires. After that time, if there are no problems the purchaser would be required to pay immediately. The contract should also describe procedures to deal with any disputes relating to invoices and payment.

Other legal issues

There are also a number of sundry legal issues that may need to be addressed in an outsourcing arrangement. Some of these are discussed below.

Occupiers' liability

In some larger contracts, the supplier will expect to have some of its staff permanently located on the purchaser's premises. There are legal issues relating to how the liability is to be split between the purchaser and the supplier if one of the supplier's employees suffers an injury or illness as a result of carrying out duties on the purchaser's site. The supplier will have a general legal obligation as an employer to provide a safe work environment, but in reality the safety of the work environment will be under the control of the purchaser. The parties will need to agree on who is liable to compensate the injured or ill individual.

Asset leases

In many outsourcing exercises, assets such as equipment are sold to the supplier and leased back to the purchaser. There are significant legal questions surrounding the structuring of the asset leases. Consideration must be given to the terms of the leases, including their duration, and what happens at the end of the life of each asset. There are also potentially complex tax and accounting implications relating to the sale and leaseback of equipment and other assets.

Conclusion

It is important to get the legal aspects right *ab initio* (from the beginning). As with any legal contract, you must approach it as though you have had a disagreement and write it from that standpoint. Writing it to rely on gentlemen's agreements will reduce fees initially but will cause insuperable problems later on. There is nothing that lawyers like more than poorly thought-through and badly defined contracts – they are just open checks for them.

Bad contracts lead to illwill later on if there is a dispute. Clear responsibilities and remedies make the process more transparent and less likely to deteriorate into a war of lawyers' letters. Realism is also a factor for consideration. Each side must be able to sell the contract to its senior management and each side must be seen to be benefiting from the relationship.

Using legal advisers with experience of outsourcing is of critical importance, as those who have not been involved in the process before, while giving best professional advice, will not be able to draw on past events and draft contracts to mitigate commonly experienced issues.

9
Human Resources

The human resources issue is one of the greatest challenges to the success of an outsourcing initiative. Ultimately, most outsourcing issues boil down to people issues. Furthermore, the importance of the human resources side of outsourcing initiatives applies worldwide. In every country where outsourcing is practiced, there is a great deal of concern about downsizing or layoffs among governments and organizations that are considering outsourcing. Successful management of human resources is an especially sensitive issue with unionized businesses and certain countries, such as Japan, which have traditionally embraced a policy of lifetime employment.

If you operate in multiple international markets, an understanding of cultural factors is vital. Social customs and traditions, language barriers and business norms are the characteristics that define the market, and have an impact on corporate industrial relations. Beyond that, however, also lie specific industry conditions, including awareness of outsourcing and requirements for technological advancement. Last but by no means least are the legal restrictions, tariffs and taxes, operating restrictions and other legal considerations that have an effect on an organization's day-to-day business.

The geographic separation elemental to the very structure of international outsourcing can create communication obstacles. The lack of person-to-person contact and fewer information exchanges can exact a toll in the form of less effective communications. As a result, outsourcing performance expectations, goals and metrics may be misunderstood by any of the multitude of stakeholders in an outsourcing arrangement, either in relation to you or your service provider.

It is important for the supplier/partner and the outsourcing organization to have shared human resources and communications aims in order to make any transition as smooth as possible. The partner needs to have an understanding – if not experience – of the outsourcer's vertical and geographic markets. A service provider without expertise in the specific vertical markets or countries where you operate may be unable to meet your firm's needs.

Guidelines for managing human resources

There are two aspects of dealing with people in outsourcing. First, there is employment law and people's legal rights. These vary from country to country. For example, in countries such as the US and Australia, staff have a contract with their employers and, provided that the contract is adhered to in terms of notice and benefits, or these benefits are bought off, then rights are considered to be observed. This cannot be done in a discriminatory way or the outsourcing company or outsourcer would be liable to action in the courts, but there is no long-term obligation to the employee.

In Europe, in particular in the European Union countries, there are special legal rights for employees who are involved in outsourcing or the transfer of staff from one employer to another (these rights also apply to mergers and takeovers). In the European Union, the Acquired Rights Directive means that employees have the right to keep their terms and conditions of service when they are transferred to an outsourcing service provider. This directive protects employees from being transferred to a new employer and losing their benefits or having their terms and conditions changed against their will. For example, employees cannot be paid less than they were previously without their agreement, their length of service is counted from the start of their original service (giving rise to bizarre anomalies such as employees of outsourcers receiving 25-year service awards when the company has only been in existence for 10 years or so) and they cannot be made redundant without being paid for the original length of service. In fact, their terms and conditions remain largely the same.

This legal aspect must be properly observed when outsourcing. Your human resources director must therefore play an active part in ensuring that people's rights are known and, in particular, that any special periods of notice or consultation are built into the overall plan. The Acquired Rights Directive stipulates consultative periods, for example, that cannot be shortened beyond a minimum period of six weeks (the interpretation of 'reasonable time for consultation'). If your HR director has never outsourced before or not done so recently, get external expertise to ensure that things are correct, as discussed in

Chapter 8. Ending up in court being sued by employees will probably outweigh any benefits of outsourcing.

The second personnel aspect is the requirement to know, and to let the service provider know, who is likely to be transferred as part of the outsourcing deal. Remember that the service provider probably needs your staff to help it run the service.

You may have thought that the service provider would use its own staff. But think this one through:

✛ What business would keep idle staff on its payroll in case they sign your contract?
✛ Anyway, how will these idle staff know anything about your business?
✛ If there are no idle staff, waiting to spring into action the day after you sign, how will the service provider begin transition?
✛ By using your staff of course – to ensure continuity of service.

Therefore the service provider will use your staff. But it should be able to manage them more effectively and provide them with better training and equipment. The service provider will be able to offer a wider range of opportunities and better career progression. The staff are moving from the periphery of your organization to the centre of the service provider's.

So you need to get your staff ready to make this transfer. We have already discussed the need to get the legal framework right. But any manager knows that there is a lot more to dealing with people than getting the legal things right.

There used to be a sales method that was credited to IBM: the fear, uncertainty and doubt (FUD) approach. So the story goes, when an organization wanted to replace its computer (we are talking huge things in controlled atmospheres) a variety of salesmen (they were mostly men, then) would come round from organizations whose names are in the history books, and try to sell their machines. The machines would do super things, but not really be so different one from another. Then the IBM salesman called. He would hum, and haw, and cast doubt on the soundness of the other machines or the other selling companies. He would introduce some uncertainty about whether now was the right time to make this new choice. He might even make the buyer afraid that other companies could not deliver as well as IBM and this would damage the buyer's organization and therefore the buyer's own prospects. The buyer, now suffering from fear, uncertainty and doubt (FUD), would take his pen and sign the IBM order while the salesman said: 'No one ever got fired for buying IBM.' It would be a great story if it were true.

But what *is* true is that people can feel FUD. They can feel that their own prospects are in jeopardy. And when they begin to feel this they think about their homes, their children and their parents who rely on them. People do not function well in this mode. They tend not to give of their very best for long when they are worried. They may begin to resent the organization that treats them like this, and begin to look around for another organization to treat them better.

They feel this FUD because there are always rumors about what is happening. To overcome this you need to communicate. Our view is that communication starts at the beginning, goes on to the end and then... goes on some more. Clearly, there are some hard messages to be given. The first response to the message 'We are thinking of outsourcing' may be a feeling of rejection: 'You don't love me any more'. But staff will probably feel this anyway, as strange people appear and ask questions, or rumors abound. So tell them – there are problems, we need to do something, outsourcing is an option, we have a process for deciding. Be clear that there are roles for the current staff in the outsourced service. If there aren't, make a plan about keeping those you need to keep for as long as you need them.

One financial services organization kept people by paying a termination bonus provided that they stayed to the end and the outsourcer took over a running service – it worked. And many of the staff were offered jobs by the service provider if they wanted them.

But clearly, just communicating in a scattergun fashion won't work. Communication must be in parallel with all the other activities, must contribute to them and be informed by them. So make a plan. Look at the strategic issues:

✤ Do you want to transfer staff? (Or, in Europe, are you obliged to transfer staff by law?) If not, how will the transition work?
✤ Are you interested in whether the service provider is a good employer for transferred staff? FI, an outsourcing group, has never made a transferred employee redundant. This is a claim it makes with pride, and one that it does not wish to jeopardize. This is a very positive message to staff – if you transfer to the outsourcing company it will want you to stay and will look after you.
✤ Does the staff issue outweigh everything else? Probably not, so you are looking for a good service provider who will meet your business objectives,

and who will be a good employer for your transferred staff. You don't want the best employer at the
expense of not meeting your business objectives.
+ Do you think staff have a role in selecting the service provider? Shreeveport's advice is not to involve
staff in the choice, but to think about getting them
to meet the selected outsourcer before or just after
contract signing. A service provider worth its salt
should have a plan of communication and winning
hearts and minds as part of its proposal.

As an example that disproves our advice, the National
Rivers Authority in the UK wanted to get a better range
of expertise and experience in designing and managing the building of flood defenses around rivers and
the sea. Its in-house design unit was small, and could-
n't really offer the career progression and breadth of
expertise that were necessary to keep excellent staff
interested. It decided to look for a service provider and
outsource the function, buying back the expertise as it
needed it.

In this public service, the workforce was strongly
unionized and was initially very alarmed by the
prospect of the change. However, in keeping with the
NRA's corporate mission statement, the outsourcing
team, including Shreeveport, involved staff representatives in the outsourcing process, allowing them to
meet potential service providers. They attended meetings as observers, or non-voting members. This
changed a very negative view into a great deal of
excitement as staff saw that the professional opportunities would be greatly increased by working in a commercial practice that dealt with more than flood
defenses. The selected service provider was accepted
by staff as a good choice and they were happy to work
in a new environment.

✣ Are there other initiatives that are being communicated to staff? Should you roll all this into one communication forum or blast staff with lots of
information?

✣ Have you thought through staff's likely questions (a
sample list is in Table 9.2 on page 167) and do you
have answers to them?

✣ How long will it take you to reach certainty about
who will be the service provider? When will the
contract be signed? What then?

✣ Can you or the HR directorate provide a hotline for
staff to call with questions? This may keep people
from worrying unnecessarily.

✣ Are there other ways to provide dripfeeds of information – regular team meetings, cascade
processes, chairman's briefings? Even if there is
nothing much to say, say that, so people know
what's going on.

✣ Are there other stakeholders that you need to
include? Shareholders, customers?

All these issues must be addressed so that you can give
staff the information they need to keep on focusing on
their jobs and delivering your service. Let them know
if decisions are imminent or a long way off. And like all
things you must do as a manager, do what you said you
would do – keep in touch and let people know of any
changes in timetable, or you will lose credibility.

Thomas Cook

When Thomas Cook outsourced its IT department to Cap
Gemini, it failed to keep staff informed, which resulted in an
atmosphere of fear, uncertainty and doubt. In a buoyant
market, specialist IT personnel had little difficulty in finding
new jobs. This put pressure on Cap Gemini's ability to

deliver the service, which in turn was potentially dangerous for Thomas Cook.

Basic change management skills are invaluable here. It is vital that the project tries to meet as many of the individuals' needs as well as keeping to key aspects of the organizational culture.

Figure 9.1 depicts the need to have all of the elements in balance – the organization and its culture, individual beliefs and attitudes, and the change program initiated by the decision to outsource.

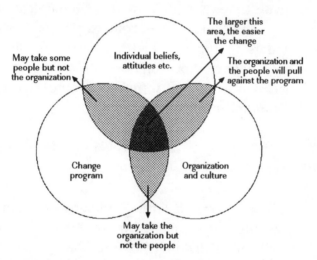

Figure 9.1 *Positioning the project for change*

Transition plan

A fundamental requirement of a well-managed outsourcing arrangements is a detailed transition plan addressing all aspects of human resources. It should deal with issues such as how individuals will be identified as staying or going to the new organization as appropriate, the benefits and policies of both the outsourcing organization and the supplier, as well as their cultural compatibility. It should include a timetable showing the key decision points and, most importantly, it should contain a detailed communications plan stretching the entire length of the intended outsourcing arrangement (i.e. several years).

This plan requires input and commitment from both outsourcer and supplier, and should be drawn up as part of the supplier selection process. This helps achieve many things: it assists the outsourcing organization in understanding the way in which each supplier is approaching the project, helps plan adequate time to implement the communications strategy, and encourages consistency and clarity of understanding across all key parties involved in the outsourcing. Above all, it will drive outsourcing management to allocate sufficient resources to the task of communication.

Stakeholders

It is imperative to consider the way in which the outsourcing arrangement will be perceived from all angles and by all stakeholders. These stakeholders are often more diverse than is imagined, and the importance (and indeed feasibility) of communicating to each separately will depend largely on the industry in which the outsourcer is operating. Table 9.1 lists some of these stakeholders.

Focus on the positive

It is also essential to project the positive aspects of being outsourced and the beneficial impact it could have on employees' careers. An IT person working for

Table 9.1 *Stakeholders*

Internal	External
Transferring employees and their representatives	Unions
Non-transferring employees in organizational proximity to those transferring	Customers
	Suppliers
Outsourced service users	
Non-service users but interested internal parties (organization wide)	Strategic partners
Management involved in outsourcing areas	Financial markets and investors
Senior and board-level management	Press
Organizational change catalysts (outsourcing project team)	

a bank will be seen as providing an essential support service, with a limited career path. Moving to an organization whose entire business is focused on the provision of information technology services allows such a person to align their personal competencies with those of the new organization and for the development of unlimited career opportunities.

The following points should particularly be borne in mind:

✛ In some industries skilled staff are in short supply. For example, in the National Rivers Authority the service provider needed design and engineering skills. Often the supplier will only be able to take over the function/service with a transfer of existing staff. This can be part of a very positive message for staff.

✛ Where management has been poor and productivity well below the industry average, staff may believe that the legislation will prevent them from needing to change their approach; this is not the case. In contrast, other groups of staff may believe that hard-won working conditions and pay above exploitation level will be lost overnight.

Conditions and benefits

Aside from the considerable communications activities that need to be planned, human resource activity in arranging an outsourcing initiative can be divided into a number of issues, an understanding of which will help answer questions that staff are likely to pose.

There are two questions that staff involved in (or close to) outsourcing ask first:

✛ Will I have a job/what will happen to my job?
✛ What will happen to my pension?

(See Table 9.2 on page 167 for some other questions that staff may have.)

It can be difficult and time consuming to identify staff to be transferred, especially when only a portion of some employees' jobs is involved. Clear and fair rules are required, not least because this can become a serious issue in a unionized environment, and because staff will want to understand why they and not others are being transferred.

Pensions planning (past service options, future service options) is very important. Not surprisingly, staff also get very concerned about their pensions – particularly those with long service. Early contact between pension scheme trustees is invaluable to discuss future service scheme replication and establish basic transfer value terms of reference for past service. Not only are staff likely to ask many questions about their pensions from the very start, but depending on the relative pension scheme benefits, this factor may have an impact on the financial business case to outsource.

Other benefits, including company car schemes (essential, benefit, personal lease) and share option schemes, also need to be analyzed carefully. In certain circumstances the specific rules of these schemes may result in a reduction in employment benefits to transferring staff. As a general rule, it is considered wise either to duplicate these benefits exactly or at least to compensate for them adequately. Otherwise, negative staff reaction should not be underestimated, and could undermine the transition to managed service.

Employee resistance

This is one of the most serious problems that will need to be overcome if the outsourcing initiative is to succeed. When a change on the scale of that demanded by an outsourcing initiative is announced it is, unfortunately, human nature to be against it. We are all conservative in nature and by and large resist change.

Outsourcing has sometimes suffered from a negative press. This is not really deserved: in many cases the initiative will boost staff careers and enrich their experience. However, it is necessary to factor the resistance into the plan and develop a way to counter it.

Essentially resistance is a vote for the status quo. Staff resist for a number of reasons:

✛ They feel that they have lost control over their jobs and possibly their lives.
✛ They are upset by the uncertainties surrounding the project.
✛ They are afraid of the difference – what will I be doing, how will it affect me, what will I have to do that I don't do now?

✦ In some cases they might fear increased workloads without any compensation.

✦ They will almost certainly feel that they have lost some power or been disenfranchised, even if this is not the case.

✦ They feel under threat, mostly because they have misunderstood the truth and paid attention to half-truths and falsehoods.

✦ Staff represent the old way of doing things and do not want to change (we tried that beforehand and it didn't work).

✦ They perceive a political threat to them – often why some managers are against outsourcing – which is sometimes not unfounded.

✦ There is a culture clash between their current organization and the new one (real or perceived).

✦ The ramifications of the outsourcing initiative haven't been explained to them.

It is not just employees who resist the change that outsourcing introduces. Managers can become a serious obstacle to the success of an outsourcing arrangement.

We have witnessed this resistance taking various forms:

✦ They are unsure about the financial benefits of outsourcing – either because many of the benefits are non-financial or because they are unhappy about the actual amounts.

✦ They feel politically threatened because their staff numbers are being reduced, or generally because they are uncertain about the potential long-term effects on them.

✦ They believe that nobody else could know their aspect of the business better than themselves.

✛ They feel a loss of control over their area of the business.

✛ They do not trust the supplier.

✛ They resist because they are daunted by the amount of work required of them to implement the outsourcing arrangement successfully, as well as the additional workload on them once transfer has taken place to 'compensate' for perceived possible failings of the supplier.

Overcoming resistance

Most of the fears and concerns of both staff and managers are misconceptions about an uncertain future. Communicating a clear picture of what will happen is therefore the primary way to overcome these concerns.

The positioning of the entire outsourcing arrangement can be quite important. Most companies that we have worked with in the past have been honest in declaring that they are entering into an outsourcing arrangement. However, they have also emphasized the 'partnership' nature of the deal in order to soften the blow, and highlighted the close working relationship that the two organizations will have in the future.

Generally, in order to engender trust, the message in all communications has to be legally correct and truthful, directly address the concerns of all stakeholders, and be available to staff as needed (in regard to both time and place). Table 9.2 contains a list of questions that need to be answered to mitigate worries.

Certain employees will not have access to certain forms of communication, and a multitude of means should therefore be employed (internal briefings, supplier roadshows, noticeboards, intranet websites, telephone helpdesk).

Another approach to reducing transfer stress is to involve employees and managers as early as possible in the outsourcing process. Understanding the supplier, their approach to service provision and transition management and their culture is key to a smooth service transition. Supplier roadshows and other meetings, both formal and informal, gently introduce employees to their future employer. User roadshows (if appropriate depending on what is being outsourced) begin to introduce key parts of the organization to their new service supplier.

Lastly, employees and managers tend to respect high-level seniority. In the most successful deals we have worked on, we have found that encouraging senior management of both the outsourcer and the supplier to be actively involved in the communication process (either as part of the announcement or the transition communications) is beneficial in achieving rapid buy-in to the process.

Table 9.2 *Typical staff questions*

Outsourcing
✣ What is outsourcing?

Business reasons
✣ Why are we seeking an IT services partner?
✣ What benefits will outsourcing bring to the company?

The partnership
✣ What is meant by a partner?
✣ Who is our chosen partner?
✣ Which companies were considered as potential partners?
✣ Which areas are being considered for outsourcing?
✣ How will the outsourcing partnership be implemented?
✣ What will the organization be like after transfer?
✣ How will the interface between company and partner work?
✣ What will happen to the management team?

Process
✣ What will happen next?
✣ What is the process of transition?
✣ What are the key stages of the outsourcing process?

The individual
✣ In practical terms, what does this mean for me?
✣ Will my current job continue?
✣ Will there be any effect on people who do not transfer?
✣ Will part-time contracts be honored?
✣ What will happen to subcontractors?
✣ Will I have to relocate if I am transferred?
✣ Will we have to move to different office accommodation on site?
✣ How will I be involved in the process?
✣ How will work be managed during the transition?
✣ What about meetings I have arranged, do I keep them?

Table 9.2 *Typical staff questions (cont.)*

✛ What if I am absent, how will I be kept informed?

✛ Will I be able to speak to anyone who has previously transferred to the partner?

✛ How will my concerns be addressed and how will I know what is happening?

✛ What happens if I do not want to transfer to the partner?

✛ Is voluntary redundancy/early retirement an option?

✛ Does the partner recognize trade unions?

✛ Are the unions involved in consultation about outsourcing?

✛ Can I stay in the union?

Terms and conditions

✛ Will my terms and conditions of employment be affected?

✛ Will we have to transfer to the partner's terms and conditions?

✛ Will I sign a new contract of employment?

✛ Could I change to the partner's contract?

✛ Will previous service be preserved?

✛ How will I be paid and when?

✛ How will my next pay review be handled?

✛ What will happen to any existing reward schemes if I am transferred?

✛ What will the implications be for those people who have cars in an employee car scheme?

✛ What is the policy on flexible working?

✛ What will happen to my pension on transfer?

Careers and development

✛ What will be the effect on my job and career development if I am transferred?

✛ What about my career prospects and planned promotion if I am transferred?

✛ What is the partner's attitude to training and development?

✛ What staff development process does the partner have?

✛ What about acquiring new skills?

Table 9.2 *Typical staff questions (cont.)*

✢ Will we continue to work on existing projects or will we be reassigned if we are transferred?
✢ What about opportunities in other locations?
✢ How are vacancies advertised?
✢ How will my performance be assessed?

General
✢ How do we handle queries from the press?
✢ How will customers/suppliers know what is happening?
✢ How should I respond to questions from customers/suppliers?
✢ When will I receive further information?

10
Implementation and Monitoring

Once the deal is signed and the outsourcing initiative is under way, there is an enormous temptation to breathe a sigh of relief and, rather optimistically perhaps, 'go back to normal'.

Market testing

During the late 1980s in the UK, the then Prime Minister Margaret Thatcher was keen to reduce the number of public servants in UK government. To achieve this she instigated a program of outsourcing (called 'market testing', meaning that the value for money of in-house services was tested against what the market would provide). This program often shook the middle managers and staff involved to their core. To be successful in retaining the service in-house massive changes were frequently required, including staff reductions and the introduction of new working practices.

Sadly, after what were radical shifts in outlook and culture for these relatively junior staff, senior managers on more than one occasion said 'Now that's over we can go back to normal', provoking a furious response. Certainly they could revert to 'normal', but a new 'norm' that included the outsourcing supplier.

The new norm means that the performance levels that were agreed as part of the bidding/negotiation process must be demonstrated and reviewed, actions taken to ensure corrective procedures are instigated when needed, and so on. In short, where once an in-house function was managed, or maybe was ignored and left to get on with it, the *contract* must now be managed. And somehow the expectation or perception of service where money leaves the organization is inevitably higher than where it is all counted as salaries and overheads.

Shreeveport's recent survey into outsourcing (the findings of which are included in the Appendix) suggested that around 42 percent of organizations have no agreed measures in place to ensure that they receive the agreed benefits from outsourcing. There was a close parallel between closely monitored benefits and industry sectors where quality management was strictly observed. The survey also showed that almost all of the measures in place were introspective, that is, they involved judgmental assessments of achievement. With the exception of user surveys, very few actually used objective measures such as benchmarks.

The transition to working with the service provider

One of the problems of embarking on an outsourcing deal is that people can have unrealistic expectations of what outsourcing will deliver. A very common mis-conception is that the level of service will change from day one after the outsourcing contract begins. This is not a reasonable expectation. For one thing, the transition to outsourced delivery may well involve people who formerly worked in-house moving to working for the service provider; they are hardly likely to perform at their best from the start. Furthermore, the outsourcing arrangement needs to be 'run in', meaning that the organization and the service provider must get used to working with each other and create the necessary synergy; this is not likely to happen overnight.

That said, it is of critical importance that the deal begins well. The initial perceptions of the new service provider will form a baseline for people's expecta-tions throughout the contract. So while service will not change immediately, one of the key criteria that must be looked for in any supplier's approach is a well-managed and thought-through transition phase.

In strategic relationships involving co-sourcing or those that are benefits based, the transition phase may encompass post-contract verification, making it all the more important that this is well planned and managed.

Key elements to look for in a supplier's transition plan are:

✣ A structured approach to any staff transfer.
✣ A realistic period of appraisal of equipment and assets.
✣ A reasonable approach to asset/equipment improve-ment through investment or better maintenance.
✣ Clear and uncluttered management structures to ensure that progress is continuously made and problems are readily identified and addressed.

Over-ambitious or over-eager transition planning may stem from a lack of experience in this area or, more worryingly, may reflect a desire to complete the deal at any cost. However, the initial impressions that your business has of the supplier that you will be seen as having recommended, if not chosen, must be good ones. The amount of work that it will take to over-turn poor first impressions will outweigh any savings or speed of change achieved.

It is difficult to put a timescale on how long a transition phase should last. It is dependent on the scale and scope of the function being outsourced. After a year or 18 months of transition, it is reasonable to say that some kind of 'business as usual' has been achieved, otherwise transition itself becomes the norm.

The implementation and monitoring process

To optimize the time and effort involved in this ex-post aspect of outsourcing, it is important that the following items are in place:

+ clear objectives
+ agreed objectives
+ performance measures to support those objectives
+ agreed sanctions for non-performance
+ agreed frequency of reviews
+ agreed dates and submissions for the reviews
+ escalation process (an arbitration agreement can be helpful here)
+ feedback and lessons learned sessions.

Clear objectives

As we have said throughout this book, you must identify and state your objectives for the outsourcing exercise. It is surprising that anyone would embark on such an exercise without being clear what the objectives are, but some do. Don't be one of them – you cannot monitor your success unless you know what you were trying to achieve.

Agreed objectives

Having identified your objectives, make sure that they are agreed – not just internally, although this is critical, but with the supplier. If you are clear about what you have to achieve and communicate this to your supplier, any proposed changes or innovations can be gauged against how they will support the objectives.

This applies in particular to change control. Mechanisms must be defined that allow either party to the outsourcing agreement to propose changes. These are not changes to the contract, which would be the subject of detailed legal negotiation and should be unnecessary during the life of the contract. Change control will manage proposed changes to the SLA, either in terms of requirement, i.e. something different should happen, or in terms of performance measures, i.e. it should happen faster or less often etc.

Change control will be a set of procedures defining the stages through which one party can propose a change, where the change is costed and other impacts defined, and where each party can consider whether to accept it and it can be agreed or rejected. The contribution or not that the change will make in achieving the objectives is a vital part of that consideration.

It may be that the supplier can think up an innovative way to improve how it meets your objectives – which is great! But do remember that the supplier has to know and understand what your objectives are in order to do this.

Performance measures

Once objectives are clear and agreed, the way that service performance will be measured should be set. If the objectives contain reference to 'world-class service', you must decide what this means. It could be, for example, that you want to be at 75 percentile or above when measuring the Fortune 500 for this service. And importantly, before setting this as a performance measure be clear if and how you will actually measure the performance.

You may also have unit cost reduction as an objective. This could be measured against your baseline information. Ultimately, you may find that because service expectations are increasing inexorably, you have to benchmark unit costs externally to define standard unit costs.

Sanctions for poor performance

There are two reasons that sanctions for poor performance exist:

✛ To recompense you and your organization for a failure on the supplier's part to deliver agreed service.
✛ To 'punish' the supplier and thereby encourage better performance in the future.

In terms of recompense, we believe that you should seek recompense that matches the loss of service you received. This would normally mean getting, say, x hours of service free of charge, when service failure meant that you were without service for x hours. Effectively, you get service credits that match the period of non-performance. It is unlikely that on an outsourcing basis a supplier will agree to making good any consequential loss.

B&Q

The do-it-yourself chain B&Q outsourced the IT systems supporting replenishment of its stores. If the system failed and the shelves were empty of pink paint, how much would B&Q have lost? How could we determine that any pink paint would have been sold if it had been there? If during this period profits dropped and as a result the share price fell, could this be attributed to system downtime and the resulting lack of paint? How much would B&Q have lost then? As we say, suppliers tend not to sign contracts giving them liability for consequential loss.

'Punishing' the supplier can be equally difficult and will depend on whether you want to do this and your muscle at the negotiating table. If a hefty fine is imposed for breaches of the SLA, then certainly the supplier's senior management will focus attention on making sure that the SLA is not breached. But this results in time arguing with you at contract management meetings about whether you fulfilled your role fully. Maybe that service breach was because your staff were five minutes late doing x or delivering y. Don't expect the supplier to accept a fine without a protest. The service delivery manager will spend a lot of time not on managing your service to give you the best to meet your objectives, but instead on protecting his or her back!

Agreed frequency of reviews

You need to get suppliers to make your life easier. Therefore, they should measure their own performance and report it to you. You should be satisfied that the supplier has good procedures in place and can ensure the quality of service, monitoring it and reporting on it. By all means build in some service sampling, but don't replicate the supplier's management function in order to measure its performance. This will cost too much to deliver too little benefit. If you suspect that performance is being misreported, then use your right of audit (you did put that into the contract, didn't you?) to check.

Meet to discuss performance at an appropriate frequency. Monthly meetings at contract manager level are usual, with quarterly or half-yearly meetings at director level, and big annual reviews where CEOs may meet. You may want weekly meetings during the first three months of transition.

Agreed dates and submissions for reviews

Having agreed the frequency it is a simple matter to schedule a year's worth of meetings, as it is particularly useful to get into directors' diaries early.

The reports that you will discuss at the reviews should be defined, and so should the time before the meeting by which you want them to arrive. There is little point in meeting if you haven't time to review the reports in detail.

Escalation process

When problems arise, it is important to have a well-defined, timed escalation process. This should include:

✦ some way of prioritizing problems so that they can be dealt with appropriately

✦ time limits for the resolution of problems, varying according to the severity of the problem – e.g. a minor problem should be resolved in five working days, a major problem within one working day

✦ rising seniority of supplier staff to deal with the problem, e.g. support staff, contract managers, director, CEO.

Eventually, if a problem is serious enough and persists, the supplier's CEO should ring your CEO to tell him or her how it will be fixed. How quickly this happens will depend on the severity of the problem.

You may want to define an arbitration process to deal with any problems where the cause is not agreed. The supplier may believe that you caused the problem, you may believe it was the supplier. If solving the problem incurs cost (it usually does), then you may need some independent way of resolving this in the hopefully rare cases where you cannot agree.

Feedback and lessons learned sessions

It is useful to build into the contract management process reviews of that process itself.

This can be coupled with, say, an annual review of performance that considers whether performance levels should change in response to business pressures or external change. There may be price implications of such changes, so it will be necessary for you to define any proposed changes and submit them for pricing and impact analysis prior to such review. The supplier may also propose changes – it may be that their greater knowledge and expertise suggest that you should or could be adopting something new to benefit your business. In this case you would also need to understand the price and other impacts before considering such changes.

Common problems

Getting a deal that is 'too good'

Many novices in outsourcing treat the process as though it is just another commodity procurement. They look for the absolute lowest price among competing bidders and then drive the price from there to rock bottom regardless of service or maintenance levels. In outsourcing, this can be a big mistake.

Quite often, certain service providers who are very hungry for a deal will let themselves be bid down to less than justifiable profit margins merely to sign the deal. In these cases, the customer almost always ends up unhappy with the service levels, and the service provider responds that it is doing the best it can, given the low margins that it is earning. In some cases, the margins may be so low that the service provider approaches the customer with the suggestion that it wants out of the long-term contract unless the customer is willing to renegotiate. In other words, it is not unheard of for service providers to over-commit to high service level guarantees and bargain pricing, whether knowingly or not. Prospective outsourcing customers have to be able to determine when they have struck a properly balanced deal with the customer.

Getting your service provider's attention

A common complaint among outsourced customers is: 'I can't get my service provider to respond or pay attention to my problems.' Although we hope for outsourcing relationships with service providers that work as close business partnerships, they don't always work out that way. This is when a well-conceived outsourcing contract might have made a difference. There are many components that should go into the due diligence process and into an outsourcing contract to ensure the customer gets the level of attention it deserves.

For example, during the negotiation process the customer should determine whether the service provider's account manager assigned to the customer will have a proper level of authority within the service provider's organization to deal effectively with the customer's problems. Many service providers will agree to include contractual provisions mandating that the account manager will be responsive to the customer. But customers often complain that although they may have a good relationship with their account manager, that manager doesn't have the seniority necessary to get an appropriate level of executive management attention within the service provider's organization.

Good service levels with real bottom-line consequences attached can make a big difference. A service provider who is not otherwise motivated will often begin to listen when contractual service level failures start affecting its profit margins. That is one important reason to take sufficient time to prepare a proper and thorough service level agreement that includes remedies such as invoice credits and termination rights. Other provisions, such as strong problem escalation procedures (to the highest management levels of the service provider), can be equally effective.

Measuring the benefits of outsourcing

This immensely important topic has to date rarely been given its due in business books. This is extraordinary – how can one possibly know that one is getting benefits from outsourcing unless one measures them?

Performance measurement is a complex area, for the following reasons:

✢ Simple measures of cost reduction or quality improvements will become less meaningful over time.
✢ Measuring against the business case may not be meaningful if the real world changes in a way that has not been assumed.
✢ There are direct benefits attributable to the service that must be measured.
✢ The indirect benefits may need a more comprehensive change program across your organization before they will be gained.

The measuring process must start with setting the objectives of the exercise at the very beginning of the outsourcing process.

Types of benefit include the following.

Cost reduction

This should be an obvious, easily definable benefit. Against the same level of service, are you paying less now (after outsourcing) than before? If, as is often the case, you didn't really measure the expenditure on the service in this way, then you should have created a cost baseline as part of your service specification and to evaluate suppliers' responses. Then get the supplier to 'measure' the costs for you, i.e. they should aggregate all these costs and provide you with a statement, in a format of your choosing, so that you can see the cost reductions that you have accrued.

Quality improvement

Sadly, while the easiest thing to measure is an 'apples for apples' cost reduction, it is actually unlikely that this is the result of outsourcing. You will probably seek some improvement in service that destroys the 'apples for apples' comparison in the short term. Your current service may be reasonable but could be better, so you will inevitably use the expertise of the outsourcer to seek an improvement in service.

Even if this is not your approach and you want to keep the same level of service, the world will change and expectations and standards of service will rise; unless the outsourcing results in different service levels, you will be left behind. In the mid-1980s we expected our PCs to use DOS (remember DOS?) and to stop everything while documents printed. These features would be unacceptable now because our expectations are growing all the time.

So you can compare costs for a while, but after the initial period comparisons against previous costs may not be relevant. You can still compare actual costs and service against the business case that justified your choice of suppliers. The business case should be modeled over the life of the contract and you can measure costs against those predicted. There is unfortunately a real possibility that the market won't operate in the way you assumed in the business case and you will gradually or suddenly deviate from the model, but at least there is some basis for measuring both cost and service levels for an initial period.

Other benefits

Benefits that are indirectly related to the outsourced service are harder to measure.

The benefit of freeing management time and energy can be difficult to estimate. If the service is outsourced successfully and there is a defined contract management structure in place, then other managers should not become involved in service issues or diverted from their core focus. This can be measured by asking managers if they are spending time managing the service, dealing with problems and resolving issues. If so, the contract management team must investigate why and improve their activities and procedures so that this ceases to be the case. Resolving problems and issues is the contract management team's job.

So we can (and should) measure the freeing of other managers' time. But the second element to the measurement is: 'Does your organization benefit from freeing this time?' If the freed time is spent drinking more coffee or having more 'smoke breaks' out on the sidewalk in front of the office, there may be little benefit to measure! It is critical to look holistically at the impact of outsourcing and the benefits to be reaped. Measuring better management focus on core activities should be set against the performance of those activities not relating to the outsourced service.

Similarly, where joint ventures, alliances or partnerships have been created, there are two types of benefits:

✛ those directly related to the joint venture, i.e. are unit costs for service reduced; are large investment costs spread over more parties, is management input contained and better management in place?

✤ those as an indirect result of the joint venture, i.e.
new business targets achieved because of better
management focus; the service making a greater
contribution to business by e.g. reducing time to
market for new products because of innovative
ideas from the 'experts' in the venture.

You should use this experience of performance to
learn as an organization how greater focus can be
applied and measurably improve corporate performance. This will mean looking at whether
individuals/divisions relying on the outsourced service should be given new, more challenging targets that
are then linked back to the outsourced service
supplier's performance. This is the development of a
benefit-based relationship.

However, the outsourced service may be only one
element that a division or manager uses to achieve
his/her targets. If they succeed only partially, what
proportion of the benefit and therefore reward do you
attribute to the outsourced service and its suppliers?
The supplier may, justifiably, say: 'If the service delivered 100 percent of what it should have, then give me
100 percent of my reward. If your manager only
achieved 50 percent of his or her target using my 100
percent service, then you should have managed him
or her better.'

The change to an outsourced supply can be far
reaching and the full range of benefits will not be
achieved overnight. A structured approach to managing the service and measuring performance is
required to ensure that you do get the benefits you
expect. An annual review will ensure that the service
remains focused on achieving your business
objectives.

Reletting the contract

So you have done outsourcing, and the T-shirt is still wearable. But the time has come for the contract to end. Now what do you do?

There are a few options open to you, but each has its limitations:

✢ Run another competition, just like the first one, and go through the whole complex process again. You may find that there is a different level of interest from potential service providers – your incumbent may be seen as being way in front of the rest of the field. Other service providers may think that because you have no particular problems with the incumbent the competition is merely benchmarking and they may not be willing to expend all the effort of producing a bid for you to compare.

✢ If things are going fairly well (but how well is fairly well?) you may think about extending the existing contract. Of course, it is not good practice to extend contracts indefinitely. There may be movements in the market that make the original deal less competitive and less attractive for your business. And if you are not particularly happy, or feel that you are unhappy, with the incumbent then maybe you want a change.

✢ One way of maintaining a sense of what's going on elsewhere is to benchmark your service provider's performance with other similar services elsewhere. There are a number of benchmarking clubs that you could join to assist you in finding suitable candidates for benchmarking, or you may have organizations in your industry or elsewhere that you know well enough to ask for benchmarking information. At Shreeveport we recommend that you benchmark throughout the contract life to maintain your awareness of the market. Some link to benchmarking results could be built into the contract to give you the ability to manage increase in price or quality with your service provider. As a result, you may decide that you need to change your contract and this might stimulate you to run a competition, or vice versa.

✤ Undertake a strategic review. Business is moving fast in all areas, technology is changing and there are new business models that need to be exploited to be successful. Who would have predicted that we would be buying children's toys over the internet by the year 2000? Before thinking about signing a new contract, think strategically – after all, this is about strategic sourcing, not tactical actions.

In the UK, government agencies have to review themselves every five years asking the following questions:

✤ Does what we do need to be done? Could we just stop and it would make no difference?
✤ If it needs to be done, do we need to do it in the public sector?
✤ If the public sector does not need to do it, how much control do we have to have over the function and the assets to do it? Can we outsource or privatize it?

Similar questions need to be asked before embarking on a further outsourcing contract:

✤ Does your organization still need the service?
✤ If so, is it the same service as is currently contracted for, or as a result of benchmarking and market surveys do you need something slightly different?

✛ Or do you need something radically different?

✛ Should you outsource this or do it in-house?

It is highly likely that the markets for both you and your service provider are changing and there may be both new needs you want to have met and new ways of delivering the service that should be taken into account.

You should certainly not sign any extension of contract or new contract without undertaking a strategic review first.

Changing service provider

When it comes to it, can you really change service provider? The answer is yes, with either careful planning or with some difficulty. We discussed in Chapter 8 the need for termination rights. This should include making the handover to a new service provider as smooth as possible. But it will still be a significant exercise to change, depending on the assets and staff that were and are involved.

Staff and assets pose two particular issues:

✛ What are you going to do about retained knowledge and skill relating to your business when you change service provider? In the first outsourcing exercise your own staff provided business knowledge to the service provider. If a new service provider takes over, where does that knowledge go? How can it be handed on?

✛ Initially you may have transferred some assets or equipment. These will be out of date or at the end of their life by the time any subsequent outsourcing happens. You must protect yourself against the service provider using proprietary equipment and

then refusing to hand over the equipment to provide the service. This can be dealt with in the contract, but it essential that you do not become more
locked in than is inevitable with long contracts.

Conclusion

Planning at the outset of the outsourcing exercise
includes not just the project but the whole life of the
contract to ensure that it runs well, meets objectives
and can be ended or renewed effectively.

Appendix: Outsourcing Surveys

The Shreeveport survey

Shreeveport recently surveyed the outsourcing practices of the UK's largest 500 organizations, with
'largest' in this context measured according to a number of financial criteria.

The survey – *Outsourcing: Winning the Benefits,
Reaping the Rewards* – was essentially a qualitative one,
although some of its findings were tabulated quanti-
tatively, and involved detailed telephone interviews
with senior executives.

Overview of findings

Of the 500 organizations contacted, 60 percent (i.e.
300) said that they had some involvement with outsourcing. Eighty-eight percent of these 300 said that
their expectations from outsourcing had been met or
exceeded: a finding that from any perspective is
extremely encouraging.

At least one executive from 103 of the 300 companies was interviewed in depth.

The main benefits that organizations involved with outsourcing considered they had derived from it were as follows:

✢ reduction in the cost of obtaining the service
✢ reduction in the headcount of the organization
✢ increased flexibility of the business enterprise.

Note, incidentally, in relation to the second point that the matter at issue here was the experience of the organization surveyed. From their perspective, headcount may certainly be reduced, but it was perfectly feasible – indeed, even likely – for the service-provider to take on additional staff to fulfill the contract, even staff shed by the principal organization.

The study also found that the nature of the benefits both anticipated and actually achieved from outsourcing varied depending on the nature and value of the service outsourced.

For high-value services such as information technology, service cost reduction was the primary benefit targeted, with high quality of service also being an important benefit demanded. By contrast, the study found that for low-value services such as catering, the primary focus was on achieving headcount and cost reductions, with little regard for other considerations.

Moving on to the actual measurement of benefits, the study showed that fewer than half of the organizations involved in outsourcing actually measured the benefits they derive from it. Furthermore, there was clear evidence that outsourcing had often been initiated by organizations that had not thoroughly costed the service. As well as this, companies had frequently not developed specifications of the service and had rarely assessed the implications of outsourcing for the rest of their organization.

The study revealed that those organizations that aimed to measure benefits received tangible rewards from doing so. Such organizations evaluated the performance of the outsourced service regularly, against set criteria including objective targets. They usually had the foresight to link performance by the service provider to payments made to it.

The most frequently mentioned factors motivating the decision to outsource were as follows, in descending order of the importance attached to them by respondents:

✢ service cost reduction
✢ headcount reduction
✢ opportunity to focus more on core business
✢ competitive strategy
✢ access to expertise
✢ improved service delivery
✢ improved quality of products or services.

In terms of the most frequently mentioned aspirations from outsourcing, the study found these to be targeted cost savings, achievement of required degree of flexibility and maintenance of service standards. Conversely, the three most frequently mentioned fears in relation to outsourcing were loss of control, the implications of job losses and human resource issues.

General summary

The study was wide ranging and detailed, and we prefer to let the findings and research speak for themselves rather than attach our own interpretation to the report.

However, the overall direction of the findings is unequivocal. This is that *an organization aiming to receive the maximum benefits from outsourcing must adopt a systematic approach to it and must above all set targets for the benefits to be achieved and then measure attained benefits, and continue measuring them.*

In other words, the survey suggests that the planning stage of an outsourcing initiative is absolutely critical to the success of the entire enterprise, and also that the whole business of outsourcing must be subjected to a rigorous contract management process ensuring that all the following points are accommodated:

✣ Outsourcing is seen from the outset as a business strategy, rather than as a one-off approach to service provision.

✣ Outsourcing is seen within the context of other business initiatives such as information technology or information systems strategies, change management programs, business process reengineering or major restructuring.

✣ Objectives to be achieved from outsourcing need to be set down with complete clarity. The service must be defined in terms of its:
  — limits and interfaces
  — inputs and outputs
  — processes
  — service standards
  — service levels.

✣ The baseline cost of the service must be accurately determined.

✣ This description must be clearly enshrined in a service specification.

✣ A service level agreement must be developed.

✣ Efficiencies within the service area prior to outsourcing must be maximized, either through business process reengineering or some other radical and fundamental method.

+ Current and future user requirements must be clearly understood.

+ User views on the potential changes as a result of outsourcing must be canvassed.

+ A communications strategy to keep all stakeholders informed must be devised and implemented.

+ The organization needs to develop an intelligent understanding of exactly what is being purchased.

+ A contract management structure must be devised, reporting relationships identified, regular and frequent meetings with the supplier scheduled and matters to be reported on prescribed.

The purpose of the survey

Introduction

More than any other recently adopted business practice, outsourcing has been subjected to rigorous scrutiny by both academic and commercial researchers from every possible angle:

+ Does it work and who has it worked for?
+ What makes it work?
+ Does it deliver on promised benefits?
+ How can an effective client/supplier split be achieved?
+ Can core services really be outsourced successfully?

These and many other questions have been presented to the marketplace and, as a result, the variety and volume of research material available mean that organizations can embark on their strategic path to outsourcing armed with an insight into others' experiences.

So why did Shreeveport conduct another study? There have been global studies, studies into particular industries, studies into the concomitant organizational behavior and studies on particular types of outsourcing such as insourcing. What new focus could shed new light on the subject?

As a manager contemplating the challenge of outsourcing, critical questions to ask should arguably include: 'How will I know if it's working, what benefits should I be seeking, what should I be measuring and how should I measure it?' It is this area of benefits and the measurement of benefits that Shreeveport identified as worthy of closer examination and scrutiny.

So, while other studies have canvassed the marketplace about the positive aspects of outsourcing, this study focused specifically on the tangible benefits and intangible value of outsourcing and the best methods of capturing and measuring those performance data. Anecdotally, outsourcing is deemed universally successful, but without success indicators there is only a shallow case to support that view.

The research

Shreeveport conducted this study to qualify specific aspects of the UK outsourcing market including:

✢ general experience, perceptions and opinions of outsourcing
✢ how outsourcing is undertaken or intended to be undertaken, i.e. the process and how it is managed, especially identifying the client/supplier split and the management of relationships
✢ perceived advantages and benefits of outsourcing
✢ methods of measuring benefits
✢ important aspects of the client/supplier relationship
✢ future outsourcing strategies.

The study comprised both preliminary and original research. The preliminary research, gathered using library indices, was obtained from published reports and provided context to the study by illuminating current trends and highlighting current issues.

Based on the research objectives and refined by the desk research, a questionnaire was designed to probe the views and perceptions of senior executives of both private- and public-sector organizations in the UK. The sample for the survey, conducted confidentially over the telephone, was a listing of the UK's top 500 organizations, as determined by financial and other performance criteria.

The survey was conducted in a way that enabled respondents to be self-selecting – if they considered themselves to have outsourced services, they qualified themselves to participate. Shreeveport secured interviews with over 100 of these organizations representating UK industry in banking, manufacturing, retailing, distribution, pharmaceuticals, transport, oil and gas, electricity and power generation, insurance, electricity and water utilities.

This appendix presents the findings of the study arranged by key research topics. In addition to this introduction and the preceding summary of the important findings and major themes, there are nine further sections, each posing and addressing a different question. Within each section, the findings are presented in narrative form and sometimes illustrated with graphic representations.

Often, the survey findings were supported by the secondary data, and indeed by Shreeveport's extensive field experience and, where appropriate, this is emphasized. Sometimes, quotes from the respondents underscore the findings and where these are of interest, they are also included but are not attributed in order to honor our promise of confidentiality.

Categorization of services

In the same way that outsourcing has different interpretations, services and functional areas within businesses are often defined differently throughout industry and sometimes within industry sectors. It is important for the purposes of understanding the findings of this study and reading this report that business service groupings are defined and categorized. Before we move on to categorizing the outsourced services, we mention aspects of the UK outsourcing market in order to describe how it is currently evolving.

The outsourcing of the full range of information services – including data center operations, data services, software development and implementation, helpdesks, hardware support and maintenance and database services – is now an established practice in the UK, as it is globally. The market is established, with many suppliers operating and purchasers from all sectors, including government. Today, the term 'IT services' is understood to cover almost all services relating to information technology.

In a similar way, financial functions such as investment and pension management, payroll and debt management, including factoring, have commonly been provided by third parties. In today's market, a much wider range of central financial and administrative services, including accounting and customer-facing services, are being outsourced to managed services providers.

Another grouping is professional services such as human resource management (including training), engineering, architecture, legal, public relations, marketing, promotion and advertising. These services will continue to be sought by organizations on a project-specific basis, but within organizations where these services have previously been provided by in-house departments, insourcing (from a related company) or outsourcing are now emerging as preferred options.

Property and site services – including maintenance, cleaning, catering, security and estate management – have been renamed in some sectors and, under the umbrella of 'facilities management' or FM, are commonly outsourced. Likewise, transport (collection and dispatch), distribution, warehousing and other supply functions have long been subcontracted services, but are now being reorganized, repackaged and outsourced.

Central to a consideration of outsourcing is the notion of 'core and non-core' and 'high-value and low-value' services. Definitions of these terms vary widely, but for the purposes of this appendix, core services are those that are fundamental to the nature of the organization's business, while non-core services are not. High-value services are those that add value and contribute to the achievement of the business's objectives and are thus strategic. Low-value services play a minor, if any, role in contributing to corporate aims. An example of a high-value service is IT, while catering is a low-value service.

This brief discussion concludes with consideration of how the supplier market has evolved. Suppliers have emerged from all sectors within industry.

To facilitate sensible analysis of the survey findings, the service groupings listed below were devised to reflect our understanding of the marketplace and these will be referred to throughout this appendix. They are:

✢ IT services, which include strategy, development, implementation, technical and user support.

✢ Finance and administration, which includes managed services, investment services, pension management, payroll, factoring, debt management, accounting and customer and other front-line services.

✢ Professional services, including training, engineering, legal and marketing.

✢ Transport and distribution, including collection, storage, warehousing, haulage and delivery.

✢ Facilities, covering property and estate management and maintenance.

✢ Site services, including cleaning, catering and security.

What are the benefits of outsourcing?

Introduction

For the purposes of this survey (and indeed this book), benefits can be defined as tangible and measurable advantages. As we have seen, there can be no doubt that outsourcing is delivering benefits to the organizations surveyed, with 88 percent of those interviewed responding positively to that question. This section considers the nature of those benefits.

Perceptions of benefits

In order to understand benefits and how they are perceived, respondents were asked first about the factors that motivated outsourcing. Figure A.1 shows the most frequently mentioned motivating factors by all respondents.

Further analysis of these responses showed that the ranking of motivating factors did not significantly vary with the different categories of services, so

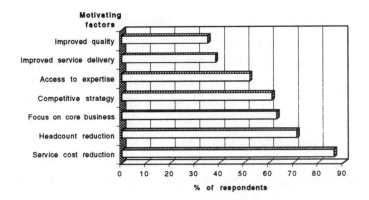

Figure A.1 *Most frequently mentioned motivating factors*

service cost reduction motivated the outsourcing of IT services as much as it did the outsourcing of site services. Service cost reduction rated most highly with all categories. Many respondents regarded head-count reduction to be implicit to service cost reduction, but nonetheless mentioned it separately. The next most important factor, focus on core business, rated strongly and it was this point that stimulated much additional comment.

One respondent recounting the motivation for outsourcing an IT service said, 'We wanted to get away from something we had neither the interest nor the energy to keep up with. We wanted to make sure that we had specialists tracking the market and ensuring that we had the best and most appropriate systems.' Another respondent from the finance sector, again referring to an outsourced IT service, stated, 'We intended to outsource everything that didn't generate revenue. For us core services are those which make us money.'

From Figure A.1, the fourth most frequently mentioned motivating factor was competitive strategy. Respondents openly stated that since their competitors were outsourcing, they believed that they risked losing ground by not following suit. The next most common factors mentioned were access to expertise, improved service delivery and improved quality. In summary, we can deduce that outsourcing is seen as a means of achieving business efficiency and of enhancing performance. Additionally, respondents viewed outsourcing as a way of tapping into expertise that would be otherwise unavailable to them; this is particularly the case with respect to the outsourcing of IT services.

Having identified the motivating factors, the survey then sought to tease out the benefits that companies experience from outsourcing. The majority of respondents, 88 percent, indicated that they believe their business experienced benefits from outsourcing. If a benefit is defined as an identifiable, measurable commercial advantage, respondents nominated many such advantages. Figure A.2 presents the benefits of outsourcing as mentioned in order of frequency.

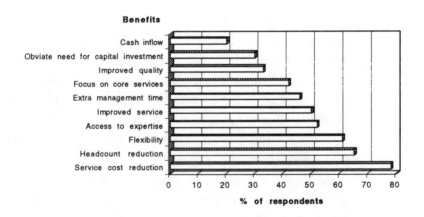

Figure A.2 *Most frequently mentioned benefits*

Overwhelmingly, the three most frequently mentioned benefits from outsourcing experienced by those surveyed were:

⁜ service cost reduction (78 percent of all respondents)
⁜ headcount reduction (65 percent of all respondents)
⁜ flexibility in terms of service delivery (61 percent of all respondents).

Figure A.2 also shows that there are two distinct types of benefits. The first are immediate benefits that may also bring secondary benefits, such as service cost reduction and headcount reduction. The other group of benefits specifically offer longer-term gains such as flexibility and access to expertise.

For emphasis, these immediate gains and longer-term benefits are separated in Figures A.3 and A.4.

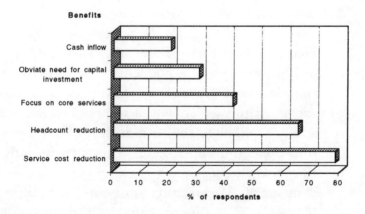

Figure A.3 *Most frequently mentioned immediate gains*

In Figure A.3, it appears that outsourcing delivers highly visible and fairly dramatic changes. Reduced costs, reduced staffing levels, surplus management time and inflow of cash from asset sales, surplus accommodation disposal or other means are all likely to have a stimulating effect on business. These are obvious benefits and are strongly linked to the motivating factors revealed earlier.

So is outsourcing a self-fulfilling prophesy? The answer is probably no. Figure A.4 shows that benefits other than up-front changes are experienced.

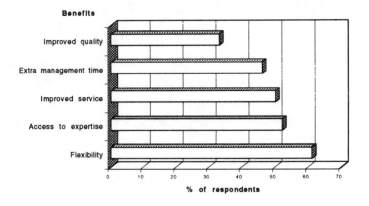

Figure A.4 *Most frequently mentioned longer-term benefits*

Figure A.4, which shows the sustained effects, demonstrates that respondents were reporting more complex benefits such as flexibility. Respondents explained this as 'enhanced responsiveness' and the ability to 'change course quickly without having to turn the entire ship around'. This is particularly pertinent when considering IT services, as one respondent stated: 'We are purchasing outcomes rather than the means of producing them so if their requirements change, we are paying for the privilege of having somebody else find and fund the new means.'

Further analysis of the benefits showed that benefits were specific to the service category. In addition to a short-term gain, service cost reduction, the emphasis is on longer-term benefits when outsourcing IT services.

The most common benefits experienced from outsourcing different categories of services were correspondingly different. For high-value services such as IT, finance and administration and professional services, outsourcing certainly does bring hard and immediate benefits such as cost and headcount reductions, but access to expertise, extra management time and flexibility are also sought. In contrast, for low-value services such as facilities and site services, service cost and headcount reductions predominate as benefits.

Our conclusion is that for high-value services, cost reductions are sought but not to the detriment of quality, while the primary focus in outsourcing low-value services is the achievement of headcount reductions without due regard for other considerations.

Respondents were also required to indicate whether they regarded the outsourced service as core to their business or not, and a majority of 73 percent saw the service as non-core. However, further analysis of this finding showed that in the instances where the respondent viewed the outsourced service as core, the service belonged to the high-value category of services, i.e. either IT, finance and administration or professional services. Many of these respondents did not distinguish between the terms 'core' and 'strategic', and we can therefore deduce that 27 percent of respondents viewed the outsourced service as critical to their business.

An interesting finding from the survey was that the benefits experienced were not specific to industry sector. This means that, for example, all those surveyed who outsource services within the category of facilities identified essentially the same benefits, regardless of whether the respondent represented banking, manufacturing or electricity and power generation. It is reasonable then to say that the benefits are not specific to the type of business but are influenced by the nature of the service outsourced.

Summary

In summary, the key drivers for outsourcing are service cost reduction, headcount reduction and focus on core business. The survey also found that many organizations outsource to maintain competitiveness. Our interpretation is that many organizations embark on the process of outsourcing without giving due consideration to the time and commitment involved and sometimes with unreasonable and unachievable expectations.

The survey found, not surprisingly, that the key benefits experienced from outsourcing were service cost reduction, headcount reduction and flexibility. The survey showed that these benefits were the same irrespective of the nature of the business, but the particular benefits were different depending on the nature of the outsourced service. So, for example, the survey revealed that the three most important benefits from outsourcing IT were service cost reduction, buying in technical expertise and flexibility, while from outsourcing facilities, the benefits were headcount reduction, flexibility and service cost reduction.

Another important finding related to the notion of high- and low-value services. For high-value services, service cost reductions were sought but not to the detriment of quality, while the primary focus in outsourcing low-value services was the achievement of headcount reductions without due regard for other considerations.

Are benefits really measured?

Introduction

This section presents the survey's findings relating to the measurement of benefits. Given that benefits are tangible qualities, it follows that measurement should be relatively easy. Despite this, our survey showed that less than half of the organizations contacted regularly measured the benefits they derive from outsourcing. We now consider this in more detail.

Measuring benefits

An overwhelming majority of respondents, 88 percent, claim to experience advantages from outsourcing. A little over half of those, just 46 percent, maintain that they do actually measure whether those benefits are accruing. This means that 42 percent of those interviewed have no evidence, other than anecdotal hearsay, to support their claim of successful outsourcing.

Figure A.5 presents a breakdown of the research sample who claim to measure the benefits of outsourced services to show where benefits are measured.

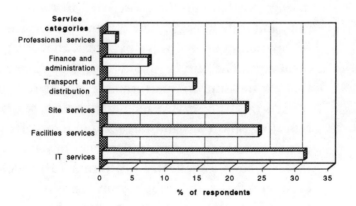

Figure A.5 *Respondents measuring benefits by service category*

Based on our sample, measurement of benefits was more common in organizations that outsourced services in the categories of IT, facilities and site services than in the other categories of transport and distribution, finance and administration and professional services.

The survey also revealed that benefit measurement was more common in manufacturing, heavy engineering, oil and gas, and electricity and power generation than in the other sectors surveyed. Businesses within these sectors, more so than others, tend to enforce more controlled and regulated work practices and operate with a stronger emphasis on quality management and performance. Quality management systems require structured and regular measurement of many metrics and it is therefore not surprising that the survey showed this trend. According to the survey, benefit measurement tended to occur less in service-oriented organizations.

How are benefits measured?

The survey has shown that fewer than half of those interviewed have instituted a rigorous method of testing the success of outsourcing. The survey also discovered that, among those who do track the outputs and outcomes of their outsourced service, there is consistency in the ways by which they gauge performance. The survey found that the organizations that do measure the performance of the outsourced service rate the service regularly against set criteria reflecting objectives and targets, and more often than not ensure that payment reflects performance.

The survey revealed different arrangements between clients and suppliers in terms of who takes responsibility for measurement and what they measure. In some cases, clients stipulated that suppliers capture and report agreed data at regular intervals, and in other cases, clients conducted the measurement themselves, with the responsibility usually falling to those in the interface role, normally the contract managers.

The survey found that the organizations that do measure whether benefits are being achieved most commonly base their measurement on the following three metrics:

✣ service objectives (55 percent of all respondents)
✣ service targets (54 percent of all respondents)
✣ user satisfaction (53 percent of all respondents).

Figure A.6 presents the most popular methods of measuring benefits.

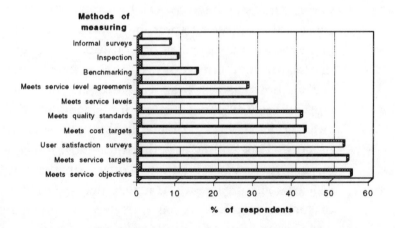

Figure A.6 *Most frequently mentioned methods of measuring benefits*

Deeper analysis of these findings showed that the most common methods of measurement did not vary significantly in correspondence with service categories. So the methods of measuring benefits of outsourcing IT services were essentially the same as those used to measure the benefits of outsourcing site services.

From Figure A.6 it can be seen that almost all of the methods are introspective, i.e. they involve making a judgment of achievement against an aspect of the service, e.g. objectives, targets, costs, levels or quality standards. There are two methods of measurement that are taken from an external point of reference: user satisfaction surveys and benchmarking.

Comparative benchmarking was undertaken by 4 percent of those who measure benefits to provide an extra dimension to the judgment of success. Comparative benchmarking is the practice of comparing certain characteristics of a service, function or process with those of the same service, function or process within a variety of organizations that are not necessarily competitors or even in the same sector. It is also known as best practice benchmarking, since it aims to identify those factors or elements of service and service delivery that contribute to successful practice. This finding is perhaps the most important because it shows that, although only a small majority, at least some organizations realize that the judgment of success in isolation has only limited application and that the process of judgment should be dynamic and based on a 'moving target', as one respondent in manufacturing and assembly asserted.

Conclusion

There is a marked contrast, then, between those organizations that do not measure benefit attainment at all and the thoroughness and rigor adopted by those that do. Our own experience and available secondary data tend to suggest that this is probably due to the influence and sophistication of the supplier sector of the market. Certainly, clients are not naive and do realize the importance of performance measurement, if only to justify their own business decisions, but they are less likely to understand the structures and mechanisms required to competently measure benefits, since this is a relatively new area for them.

Supplier organizations, on the other hand, are aware that their businesses will only grow and prosper if they can provide a service that meets or exceeds expectations and therefore measurement of their performance is critical to their case. They very often advocate performance measurement and facilitate this by suggesting measurement methods and proposing formats for regular meetings that require certain metrics to be gauged at regular intervals.

We believe that the measurement of benefits should be undertaken by clients and based on an assessment of whether the service:

✤ addresses the requirements of the service level agreement
✤ meets the service users' expectations
✤ reflects contemporary operational or functional models and incorporates appropriate elements of comparative best practice.

Leveraged benefits: what they are and why they matter

Introduction

In addition to bottom-line improvements, innovations in service delivery and detectable quality improvements, other less tangible, but nonetheless real, advantages are also experienced from outsourcing. The term 'leveraged benefits' describes these intangible benefits accompanying the implementation of outsourcing. These benefits are not less important than the primary benefits already discussed but rather, in the view of the respondents, can enhance the value of the exercise. This section discusses these extra benefits that organizations experience from outsourcing.

Leveraged benefits

Outsourcing has resulted in many changes within the organizations surveyed, not all of which are positive and not necessarily within the part of the organization that was outsourced. Many respondents spoke of the fear and anxiety that the decision to outsource created within their businesses. These fears centered on human resource issues such as job losses and job redefinition, process and procedural change, altered reporting relationships and loss of 'collective company intelligence', to quote a senior insurance executive.

Another common observation was that outsourcing is not regarded as a 'one-off but rather an approach which may take over everybody's patch', which was interpreted by many as, to use the words of a manufacturing manager, 'living in times where nobody's job is safe or certain'.

In the same way that outsourcing is seen as a threat by some, many respondents saw and continue to see outsourcing as a positive and exciting opportunity. Respondents see outsourcing as a means of driving efficiencies through their businesses, improving service delivery and ultimately enhancing customer services. This is best summed up in the words of a respondent from the banking and finance sector, to serve to focus the business on 'doing what it does best' and not struggle with areas 'where it is neither expert nor any good'.

In this spirit, many leveraged benefits, most of which were unexpected, have been experienced as a result of outsourcing. These include:

✢ acting as a catalyst for change by highlighting the need for improvements elsewhere in the organization
✢ challenging, aiding and supporting other business initiatives such as IT implementations, process modeling and business process reengineering
✢ initiating or fueling cultural change by educating people about creative service delivery options
✢ stimulating critical business analysis because of the requirement to document business processes and their costs
✢ causing a focus on the costs of services when alternative sourcing becomes a reality
✢ where it is working well, providing a strong case for the introduction of outsourcing to other areas of business
✢ invigorating businesses by converting sometimes sluggish functional areas into dynamic, successful ones and thereby stimulating internal competition and pride.

Conclusion

The survey threw light on many instances where outsourcing had positive secondary effects cascading throughout organizations and is best summed up in the words of one senior utilities director: 'Outsourcing IT had made us realize that we needed to get a handle on all of our costs and to get our house in order before we outsourced other areas. We managed to increase efficiency by up to 25 percent in other areas as a result of what we learned from the IT experience.'

How does the outsourcing experience measure up against expectations?

Introduction

Consideration of the benefits derived from outsourcing is only meaningful if done within the context of expectations. This section explores the 'softer' side of the outsourcing experience to discover whether or not outsourcing met, fell short of or exceeded expectations.

What was expected from outsourcing?

Outsourcing has been a memorable experience for the majority of those surveyed. In the words of one respondent from the food processing sector, 'We didn't know it but we started a rollercoaster that became unstoppable. It's had its highs and lows but we've all enjoyed the ride!'

The survey probed respondents' aspirations and fears from outsourcing and Figures A.7 and A.8 depict the range of expectations.

Anticipation of outsourcing served to focus respondents' thoughts on whether:

+ savings would be delivered
+ the required flexibility would be achieved
+ the service standards would be maintained
+ users would be satisfied
+ service delivery methods would be improved.

Figure A.7 shows the proportion of respondents who expressed these and other common hopes.

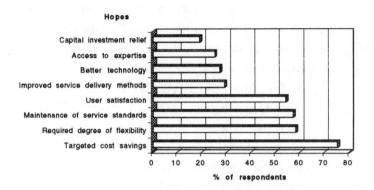

Figure A.7 *Most frequently mentioned aspirations from outsourcing*

Figure A.7 shows that the aspirations tend to match the motivating factors that drove outsourcing in the first place: that promised service cost savings would be delivered, service improvements would be achieved etc. Further analysis revealed that the importance of these hopes did not alter according to the category of service outsourced. So, expected savings were just as important to those who outsourced IT as those who outsourced transport and distribution or site services. In the same way, flexibility was equally important to those who outsourced finance and administration or professional services.

One quote does stand out as best representing the positive attitude expressed by many: 'I have no fear of outsourcing now – that's old hat. The sorts of traditional worries people have had about outsourcing, including the outsourcer not having a knowledge of their company, confidentiality and protectionism are a lot of old garbage and baggage. Those worries went out with the ark.'

Respondents were also asked about their greatest hope and whether that had been realized. Expected cost savings emerged as the most common hope (65 percent of all respondents) and 72 percent of those respondents claimed to have achieved their goal. This means that in 7 percent of cases, the expectations of respondents had not been met.

Other frequently mentioned aspirations from outsourcing were to:

✛ allow the company to focus on core activities (2 percent of respondents)
✛ spend less time involved in managing and delivering the service (1 percent of respondents)
✛ introduce innovation in service delivery methods (10 percent of respondents)
✛ provide solutions for service delivery problems (8 percent of respondents)
✛ instill discipline and predictability in service delivery (5 percent of respondents).

Figure A.8 shows the most commonly-held fears about outsourcing. These fears are presented below in descending order of the frequency with which they arose:

✛ loss of control, particularly financial control
✛ dealing with the implications of legislation and job losses
✛ managing and responding to staff reactions
✛ the ability to contain costs
✛ spending too much time in establishing the set-up
✛ becoming too reliant and dependent on the supplier.

Figure A.8 shows that most fears regarding outsourcing related to aspects of the future relationship that could not be defined, e.g. cost containment, amount

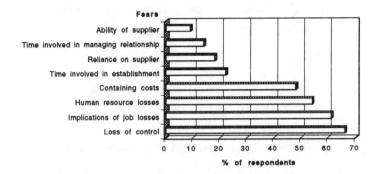

Figure A.8 *Most frequently mentioned fears from outsourcing*

of time involved and the supplier's ability. To a lesser extent, fears were also expressed about potential future conflict, e.g. job losses and other 'people' issues.

With respect to the most common anxiety, loss of control, respondents reported pleasingly that their fears had not been realized in the majority of cases. A very small percentage of respondents, 1 percent, did not have their fears relating to control allayed.

Some quotes here will help to explain the fears further. A senior director from a major media corporation said, 'When you outsource, you are reliant on their management having the same goals as you.' A power company executive remarked, 'We wondered if our outsourcing partner had the capability, knowledge, skills and attributes to handle something so complicated and so strategically important to our company.' These quotes typify the responses received.

Another key finding in relation to expectations was that the majority of respondents, 82 percent, believe that the potential exists to derive greater benefits from outsourcing. Tellingly, all respondents who believe that they are accruing benefits from outsourcing also believe that latent opportunity exists for more benefits.

Summary

Expected cost saving was the most common hope from outsourcing and around three-quarters of respondents claimed to have achieved their financial goals. The survey showed that most fears related to aspects of the future relationship that could not be defined, e.g. cost, time and ability and, to a lesser extent, potential future conflict. With respect to the most common anxiety, loss of control, 78 percent of respondents reported that their fears relating to control were allayed.

The analysis showed that there were no significant correlations between expectations and service categories or industry sectors, so hopes and fears were the same for all those who outsource.

On the question of whether potential exists to increase the benefits from outsourcing, we can deduce from the findings that all of those organizations that judge outsourcing to be a success also believe that it could be more successful.

Contract management: the hot topic

Introduction

Contract management methods and practices are becoming familiar to many managers involved in outsourcing. The survey showed that one of the most frequently mentioned implications of outsourcing was the degree of time and effort required to manage the relationship successfully, and most managers had not anticipated this. This section explores this and other aspects of contract management.

Relationships with suppliers

Some of the fanciful dreams of those who have out-sourced services were expressed during the survey:

+ 'relieving my hassles'
+ 'instilling some method into the madness'
+ 'elevating standards while reducing costs'
+ 'I wanted it to be a seamless takeover.'

Given the vagueness of many of these dreams, it is hardly surprising that many have turned to night-mares. Overly optimistic expectations were expressed by many respondents, but remembering that only 7 percent of respondents failed to have their expectations met means that the path to success for some was probably a long and tortuous one, given the sorts of aspirations listed above.

So, what's the secret? How is it that respondents who want to wave a magic wand, including the four whose remarks are reproduced above, eventually give the exercise the seal of approval?

Invariably, respondents talked about contract management as the key to successful outsourcing – and contract management in its broadest interpretation, not just the day-to-day dealings with a supplier. Before we consider how to best approach contract management and what the key success factors are, let us consider some interesting findings about attitudes to suppliers.

Over 75 percent of respondents indicated general satisfaction with their supplier. We ranked the aspects of the supplier relationship that respondents indicated were strengths, and found that the following five elements emerged in order of popularity:

+ ability to meet required service standards and levels

✛ good interpersonal relationships
✛ service delivery methods
✛ standard of communication
✛ knowledge of their own business.

Figure A.9 presents these perceived strengths of the relationship with the supplier.

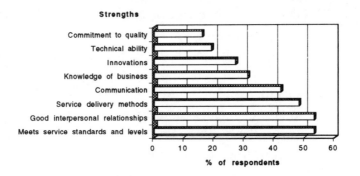

Figure A.9 *Most frequently mentioned strengths about supplier relationship*

These strengths all relate to the way the supplier does its job.

In contrast, the five elements of the supplier relationship with which respondents were least happy were:

✛ amount of time and effort required by in-house managers
✛ level of technical expertise
✛ conflict resolution and escalation procedures
✛ adversarial, commercial relationship
✛ lack of joint strategic and corporate objectives.

These factors are presented in Figure A.10.

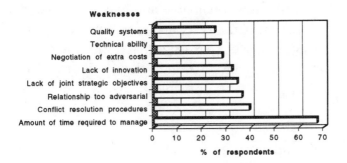

Figure A.10 *Most frequently mentioned weaknesses in supplier relationship*

These weaknesses all relate to the way the supplier manages what it is doing.

It is obvious that, when an in-house service provision team is replaced, there will be some uncertainty about the new interface and working relationship. This is supported by the findings presented above, where it can be interpreted that respondents are pleased with performance-oriented factors yet unhappy with management issues. It could be deduced that the benefits are desired for less organizational cost.

Principles of good contract management

Bearing these findings in mind – that the client perceives the supplier's abilities to manage as a weakness – it is not surprising that respondents talked about the effort they are giving to 'adopting a contract management philosophy from board level down', defining the required contract management roles and ensuring that adequate training is provided to all of those who have a critical interface with the supplier.

A frequent comment was that the amount of time required to deal with the new arrangement was much greater than anticipated and in coming to understand why that is the case, managers unearthed the important underlying reason that 'outsourcing seems to have so many fits and starts'. Respondents have found that the principles of good contract management were:

✤ understanding the limits and costs of the service
✤ having a clear basis from which to operate, either a contract or service level agreement that sets out succinct objectives, service levels and standards
✤ clear management structures and reporting relationships
✤ clear channels of communication
✤ regular and frequent meetings
✤ mechanisms for changing and adapting aspects of the arrangement.

Based on Shreeveport's experience, it is clear that a properly constructed specification of service requirements would provide a solid foundation for the development of an approach to contract management that would adhere to the principles above. It is our view that contract management works best where clarity of service requirement exists and 'legaleze' doesn't get in the way of delivering the service.

There was unison on the point that devising an appropriate contract management structure and method does take time, but when it is organized properly and appropriately, it pays dividends.

The words that respondents used to describe good relationships with suppliers included 'partnership', 'joint approach' and similar expressions intimating a mutually agreeable sharing of responsibilities. There were far more instances of respondents describing that their supplier relationships were partnerships than proved to be the case. The vast majority, over 90 percent, of respondents indicated that their supplier was not proactive in improving the service. These respondents did expect this of suppliers, so there is a clear example of where suppliers have an opportunity to work in tandem with their clients for mutual benefit.

A small minority of respondents operated shared risk/shared reward and incentive-based payment schemes or linked payment for services to performance, and the survey did find that many respondents are keen to enter into such arrangements. It appears that there is great scope for clients to innovate when negotiating with suppliers to approach true partnership models.

The survey did reveal some very interesting approaches to the relationship and payment. One organization with a large portfolio of empty commercial property pays a fixed fee relative to the floor area of all space disposed of, either through letting or sale of leases. Other examples given included arrangements where payment was linked to user satisfaction indices and bonuses being payable dependent on month-on-month efficiency improvements.

Clearly, experimentation and inventiveness are evident in the marketplace, but the survey did not find that this was widespread. From our own experience, these schemes are difficult to set up and require a great deal of time to devise and implement before they work well for both parties. This finding is therefore not surprising.

Conclusion

In summary, good contract management is regarded by respondents as implicit in successful outsourcing. The principles of contract management are not likely to be entrenched in common management practice, but rather represent a new discipline to most managers. Respondents who were managing their supplier relationships well stressed that successful contract management is underpinned by a clear and robust understanding of the costs, boundaries and requirements of the service. Again, the development of specifications of service requirements is an acquired skill, but does not necessarily require a heavy legal focus.

The survey found that the majority of respondents were satisfied with their suppliers, but there was ample room for suppliers to innovate and work more closely with their clients to effect improvements to their service delivery methods. Finally, while respondents regarded themselves as working in partnership with their suppliers and expressed this as a desire, the evidence suggests that the relationships were far more traditional and were governed by straightforward contractual arrangements.

There is great scope for these relationships to embrace the concepts of shared risk/shared reward, open book accounting and strategic objective sharing.

So that happened to you too? Common experiences

Introduction

Surprisingly, the survey revealed that respondents from all types of businesses faced the same issues when investigating, implementing and managing outsourced services. This section presents tactics that managers can consider when considering outsourcing.

The challenges

From the survey a list of common issues emerged with which a surprising large number of respondents were faced, either prior to outsourcing or following its bedding down. These issues have been consolidated and converted here almost as a 'how to' guide.

The first group of issues raised by respondents are common mistakes made by first-time outsourcers. These are the lessons that respondents would heed if they had a chance to do it over again.

The sorts of misjudgments that respondents made include:

✛ not anticipating the time required to set up for outsourcing
✛ not preparing the service for outsourcing
✛ confining the outsourcing initiative and excluding it from other business decisions
✛ failing to agree firm objectives to be achieved from the process
✛ preparing incomplete or inadequate specifications
✛ not costing the service properly
✛ not communicating appropriately with all stakeholders
✛ not instituting a means of satisfactorily managing the arrangement.

Guidelines arising from the survey

After careful consideration of the matters arising within this survey, Shreeveport has developed a set of generic guidelines for managers to follow before they outsource.

Many of these guidelines are discussed in detail in this book, but it is useful to summarize them here. They are as follows:

✛ Regard outsourcing as a business strategy, rather than a one-off approach to service provision.
✛ Consider outsourcing within the context of other business initiatives such as information technology/

information system strategies, change management programs, business process reengineering or major restructuring.

✤ Set objectives to be achieved from outsourcing.
✤ Define the service in terms of its:
  — limits and interfaces
  — inputs and outputs
  — processes
  — service standards
  — service levels.
✤ Accurately determine the baseline cost of the service.
✤ Enshrine this description in a specification of service requirement.
✤ Develop a service level agreement that prescribes a sound performance management method.
✤ Maximize efficiencies within the service area prior to outsourcing, either through business process reengineering or some other radical method.
✤ Understand current and future user requirements.
✤ Canvass users' views on the potential changes from outsourcing.
✤ Develop a communications strategy to keep all stakeholders informed.
✤ Create, structure and strengthen the 'intelligent purchaser role' and understand what is being purchased.
✤ Devise a contract management structure, identifying reporting relationships; schedule regular and frequent meetings with the supplier and prescribe what is to be reported on.

For those who have already outsourced a service, it's not too late to learn from others' experiences. The survey revealed a second group of more complex ongoing issues specifically relating to the relationship with the supplier and the service. Again, we have considered these issues and developed a set of measures that can be implemented to improve any existing outsourcing arrangements.

Examples of these issues include:

+ Identifying the wrong or inappropriate performance indicators.
+ Receiving many complaints from the users of the service.
+ Not having a mechanism to ensure that the service is improved continuously.
+ Allowing the legal issues of the relationship to govern.
+ Measuring benefits and performance from an internal perspective only.
+ Not providing enough scope in the contract for changes throughout the course of the relationship.

The following set of measures have been developed to provide guidance to managers who have already outsourced services and are seeking ways of deriving more from their arrangements:

+ Identify tangible indicators and devise a method to monitor them and measure them to track performance.
+ Demand that the supplier innovates and identifies ways of improving the service.
+ Conduct regular surveys among service users to gauge levels of satisfaction.
+ Enhance your supplier relationship by provoking discussion about the pros and cons of shared risk/shared reward and true partnership approaches.
+ Conduct some comparative benchmarking and learn what is best practice is your specific area.

✛ Renegotiate the deal when it comes up for renewal, making sure that performance will be linked to payment.

The acid test: would respondents outsource again?

Introduction

In the main, the experiences of those surveyed with respect to outsourcing have been very positive ones. In the words of one senior utilities executive, 'The company won, the supplier won and the staff won.' A good test of whether a business strategy has been successful is whether it would be implemented again, and so the analysis sought to explore links between respondents' reactions to the overall experience and their future intentions. This section sets out those findings.

To outsource again or not?

The majority of respondents reported outsourcing to have been a positive experience for their organization as judged from two perspectives: 88 percent of respondents indicated that they believe they are experiencing benefits from outsourcing, and expectations of outsourcing have failed to be realized for only 7 percent of respondents.

Typical quotes from respondents in this regard are:

✛ 'We had the service delivered to the appropriate quality at an appropriate price and at an appropriate time.'
✛ 'The service we get is first rate.'
✛ 'I'm happy to take an eyes on, hands off role.'
✛ 'There are always teething problems which for us have sorted out as time has passed and that's down to sheer commitment on our part and theirs (the suppliers).'

✛ 'We are able to respond to our customers more quickly.'

To balance this, the most common negative statements about outsourced services concern the amount of time involved in dealing with the supplier, complaints from users, the speed with which operational difficulties are resolved and the time it took to get the outsourced service up and running.

A landslide majority of 92 percent of respondents who indicated that outsourcing has been a successful venture for them also indicated that they foresaw pursuing outsourcing of other services within the next five years. Interestingly, while IT services are already well outsourced, this is seen as the largest area of growth in the market.

In closing, one quote from a senior City-based banking executive was: 'We'd do it again tomorrow but we'd never realize the same level of savings because the service would be more efficient to start with.' This imparts an important message – suppliers shouldn't be expected to realize all the benefits, preparation is important and it should be approached as a joint effort with the client and the supplier working hand in hand.

Conclusion

We conclude that the majority of companies interviewed would outsource again. The experience has been positive for the majority and 72 percent of respondents had their expectations met or exceeded by the experience.

A glance into the crystal ball: what could the future hold?

Introduction

The nature of doing business changed at an increasingly rapid pace during the second half of the twentieth century. This section is given over to how the organizations surveyed see their organizations developing and changing in the near future.

Tomorrow's organizations

Today's business visionaries foresee that tomorrow's organizations are likely to bear little resemblance to the twentieth century's commercial and industrial giants. Instead of sprawling commercial cathedrals housing many workers who provide a range of services specific to their own operation, we are more likely to see industry players as small outfits staffed by the minimum number required to deliver core services, interlocked with supplier organizations providing the same types of services to many clients.

Headlines in the 1960s and 1970s heralded the evolution of supercomputers anticipated to assume the more mundane of human responsibilities, resulting in a population of humans at endless leisure. Remember? Computers will result in the paperless office. Robots will take over most repetitive duties. But actual events have revealed these to be pipedreams.

The gurus of the 1990s also promised hope to the multitudes in the form of total quality management and business process reengineering. These, they claimed, would eliminate waste, rid us of nonsensical processes and double handling and make rejects a thing of the past. These methods were sold as being as easy to implement as waving a wand. The gurus promised that organizations would be streamlined so smoothly that they would glide on like ocean liners. BPR would turn organizations upside down and inside out. TQM would be the modern-day business bible. Were any of these promises fulfilled? The jury is still out.

And so we move on to outsourcing. What should its headlines read? They should certainly be more sober, more controlled and more in keeping with the restraint of the 1990s as opposed to the exuberance of the 1980s or the future-awe of the 1970s.

Outsourcing does make economic sense and it can be applied to all services, be they core or non-core, strategic, tactical, support or ancillary. Are we claiming that outsourcing is a panacea? Certainly not, but if applied judiciously it will result in the 'virtual office', where organizations will be physically reduced to senior decision makers and key staff providing core services.

This vision is shared by several respondents, particularly in pharmaceuticals, where one senior executive was quoted as saying that he saw his future office as consisting of 'the board and the patent department'. A respondent in heavy engineering and construction reported that their future business would 'consist only of those bits that generate revenue and we will give the rest away'.

Yet another respondent who has already outsourced IT services stated: 'We will stick to what we do best and integrate with others who do the things that we don't do well better than we can.' One media executive said, 'Oh, outsourcing, we've always done it that way. Our publishing house is me and a few colleagues in an office but my wider organization includes over 20 suppliers. I spend my life on the telephone.'

It appears that outsourcing will be responsible for introducing dramatic and highly visible innovation to the structure and focus of tomorrow's organizations.

Future outsourcing intentions

The survey questioned respondents on their current and likely future outsourcing intentions. The results showed that there will be significant growth, particularly in the outsourcing of core processes.

Conclusion

Outsourcing is here to stay. The survey indicates that it is well on the way to becoming as familiar a corporate practice as business process reengineering or benchmarking. The survey also revealed that companies considered that the practice of outsourcing would contribute to the evolution of the working environment by reducing the numbers and types of services and functions provided by businesses and by concentrating their efforts on what they regard as core activities.

Likewise, the growth of suppliers' organizations will see the emergence of many single-function, specialist entities.

The survey showed that the future of outsourcing is secure and that over the next five years, companies are likely to outsource more, especially central, core services, and fuel existing growth in the outsourcing of IT services.

The Outsourcing Institute Survey

The US-based Outsourcing Institute, which has 18,000 members, does a great service to all organizations with an interest in outsourcing by collating extensive information about outsourcing and making it available at www.outsourcing.com. In 1998 it conducted a survey of 600 of its corporate end-user members regarding their perspectives on outsourcing.

Reasons for outsourcing

The survey found the 10 most important reasons for outsourcing to be as follows:

+ To accelerate reengineering benefits.
+ To gain access to world-class capabilities.
+ To obtain a cash infusion.
+ To free resources for other purposes.
+ The organization sees the function as difficult to manage or out of control.
+ To improve the corporate focus.
+ To make capital funds available.
+ To reduce operating costs.
+ To reduce risk.
+ The organization does not have the resources available internally.

Areas in which outsourcing is currently popular

About 60 percent of those questioned were senior executives. They represented what the Institute describes as 'almost every industry', from advertising and brewing through government and healthcare to manufacturing and utilities. Their organizations ranged from small (under 499 employees) to very large (more than 10,000 employees).

By far the most active areas where outsourcing was taking place were information technology, operations and logistics. Within these areas, the specific functions either already outsourced or being considered for outsourcing were as follows:

Information technology

'This is the fastest growing area for outsourcing today,' the Institute commented. According to the survey, executives are currently outsourcing:

+ maintenance/repair
+ training
+ applications development
+ consulting and reengineering
+ mainframe data centers.

They are considering outsourcing:

+ client/server
+ networks
+ desktop systems
+ end-user support
+ full IT.

Operations – administration

Executives are currently outsourcing:

+ printing and reprographics
+ mailroom
+ consulting and training.

They are considering outsourcing:

✛ records management
✛ administrative information systems
✛ supply/inventory
✛ printing and reprographics.

Customer service

Executives are currently outsourcing:

✛ field service
✛ field service dispatch
✛ telephone customer support.

Executives are considering outsourcing:

✛ customer service information systems
✛ field service dispatch
✛ telephone customer support.

Finance

Executives are currently outsourcing:

✛ payroll processing
✛ purchasing
✛ transaction processing
✛ general accounting.

Executives are considering outsourcing:

✛ taxes.

Human resources

Executives are currently outsourcing:

✛ relocation
✛ workers' compensation
✛ recruiting/staffing.

Executives are considering outsourcing:

✢ consulting and training
✢ human resource information systems.

Real estate and physical plants

Executives are currently outsourcing:

✢ food and cafeteria services
✢ facilities maintenance
✢ security.

Executives are considering outsourcing:

✢ facilities management
✢ facilities maintenance
✢ facilities information systems.

Sales and marketing

Executives are currently outsourcing:

✢ direct mail
✢ advertising
✢ telemarketing.

Executives are considering outsourcing:

✢ reservation and sales operations
✢ field sales.

Logistics

The Institute comments: 'For any type of company that requires high level distribution or transportation, outsourcing these functions can show immediate and dramatic return on investment.'

Distribution

Executives are currently outsourcing:

+ freight audit
+ consulting and training
+ freight brokering
+ leasing.

Executives are considering outsourcing:

+ warehousing
+ distribution and logistics
+ information systems
+ operations.

Transportation

Executives are currently outsourcing:

+ fleet management
+ fleet operations
+ fleet maintenance.

Executives are considering outsourcing:

+ fleet operations
+ fleet maintenance.

Index

A

Abbey National 3
acquisitions 8, 11
administration, outsourcing
    198, 203, 205, 206, 213,
    232
alliances 183
Amazon 34–5
ancillary services, outsourcing
    6, 26, 41, 229
Andersen Consulting 14, 22
approaches to outsourcing
    6–8, 37–49, 52–76
arbitration process 178
asset leases 149–50
auditing 147–8, 177

B

B&Q 176
Bank of England 20
Baric 19
baseline 63–4, 83–7, 113–14,
    115, 175, 181, 192, 224
BBC 45
benchmarking 84–7, 141,

171, 175, 185–6, 208,
    225
benefit-based relationships 8,
    46–8, 49, 128, 172, 184
Benefits Agency 128
benefits of outsourcing x, 6, 8,
    11–12, 15, 17, 34, 37, 47,
    70–71, 78, 88, 100, 113,
    127, 129, 160, 164, 171,
    181–4, 190, 193, 194, 198,
    225, 226, 227
benefits, leveraged 12, 209–12
boundaries of outsourcing 55,
    67, 78, 112, 222, 224; *see
    also* scope
British Airways 2
British Forces 109, 124
buildings maintenance, out-
    sourcing 20, 41
business case 57–76, 93, 97,
    121, 181, 182
business processes 35

C

Cap Gemini 159

Capita 3
capital 10, 11, 201, 213, 231
catering, outsourcing 5, 20,
    35, 41, 190, 197, 198
change control 96, 174, 220,
    225
changing service provider
    187–8
chore functions 35–6
cleaning, outsourcing 5, 6, 35,
    41, 140, 197, 198
collaboration 11, 15, 22, 96
communication 14, 40, 83,
    90, 91, 95, 97, 100, 102,
    129–30, 137, 152, 155–8,
    160, 165–6, 193, 218, 220,
    223, 224
competitiveness 5–6, 199, 204
Computel 19
computer bureaux 19
concept of outsourcing 2–18
confidentiality 146–7
Conoca 23
consequential loss 176
context
    internal 77–87
    strategic 67–9
contingencies 90
contract 5, 14, 16, 44, 46, 82,
    96, 100, 107, 116, 128,
    132, 133, 134–49, 174, 180,
    182, 186, 188, 220, 222
    contingent 5
    extending 185
    management 16, 91, 104,
    108, 115, 117–18, 123, 171,

176, 178, 183, 192, 193,
    216–22, 223, 224
    management team 100–1,
    126–7
    negotiation 79, 91, 95,
    101–3, 133, 134, 136, 140,
    142, 143, 180
    reletting 185–7
    renegotiation 141, 226
    termination 116, 139, 142
contracting out 6–7, 41, 49,
    95
Co-operative Bank 2–3
core activities 9, 10, 11, 23,
    33, 36, 42, 82, 183, 191,
    193, 197, 199, 203, 204,
    214, 228, 229, 230
corporate purpose 31–2
co-sourcing 5, 7–8, 22–4, 32,
    45–6, 49, 82, 172
cost reduction 10, 11, 12, 13,
    15, 25, 41–4, 54, 67, 70,
    71–2, 81, 93, 113–14, 175,
    181–2, 190, 191, 199,
    201–4, 208, 211–16, 219,
    220, 222, 231
CSC 21, 22–4
cultural factors 120, 151, 166
customer satisfaction 2, 3, 10,
    15
customer service, outsourcing
    4, 233
customers, relationship with
    33–5, 36, 82

D

data collection 85–7, 98, 102
debt management, outsourcing 5, 196, 198
delegation 30
dispute resolution 135, 219
distribution, outsourcing 197, 198, 205, 206, 213, 235
due diligence 96, 114, 133, 180
Dun and Bradstreet 4
DuPont 22–4

E

e-business 11
economies of scale 25, 42, 43, 67
Economist Intelligence Unit 10, 17
EDS 10, 21, 47, 102, 116–17, 129
efficiency 17, 52, 200, 210, 212
employment conditions 162–3
employment law 152–3
engineering, outsourcing 20, 196, 198, 206, 229
escalation procedures 173, 177–8, 180, 218
estate management, outsourcing 5, 197, 198
European Space Agency 3
evaluation
  of suppliers 99, 100, 120–23
of performance 98, 108, 115, 117, 125, 181
exception control 102
expectations 212–16
expertise, access to 11, 14, 24, 29, 33, 37, 42, 43, 93, 109, 157, 178, 182, 191, 200–4, 213, 218, 231
extending the contract 185

F

facilities management, outsourcing 5, 20, 40, 41, 132, 197, 198, 203–6, 234
factoring, outsourcing 5, 196, 198
fear, uncertainty and doubt (FUD) 154–9
feedback 173, 178–9
FI 156
finance, outsourcing 35, 196, 198, 203, 205, 206, 213, 233
financial viability of service provider 144–6
flexibility ix, 33, 10, 11, 15, 190, 191, 201–4, 212, 213
Ford 9

G

Gate Gourmet 2
GE Capital Bank 21
General Insurance Standards Council 97

growth of outsourcing 3, 4,
    19–36
guidelines for outsourcing
    223–4

H

Halifax 10
headcount reduction 11, 190,
    191, 199, 201, 203, 204
human resource issues 82–3,
    151–69, 191, 210, 215
human resource management,
    outsourcing 4, 35, 196,
    233

I

IBM 21, 31, 154–5
ICL 21
IDC 4
information technology, out-
    sourcing 4, 5, 20–21, 22–4,
    35, 48, 86, 116–17, 132,
    140, 143, 145, 159, 176,
    190, 192, 196–8, 199, 200,
    202–3, 204–6, 208, 211,
    227, 229, 230, 232
innovation 30, 124, 209, 214,
    218, 219, 222, 225, 229
Insolvency Service 122
insourcing 5, 7, 21, 194, 197
internal context 77–87
investment management, out-
    sourcing 196, 198

J

joint ventures 5, 32, 183

K

KPMG Consulting 13

L

legal aspects of outsourcing
    95, 131–50, 151, 152–3,
    225
legal services, outsourcing
    196, 198
leveraged benefits 12, 209–12
limitation of liability 143–4
locked room method of nego-
    tiation 101
Lockheed Martin 36

M

Maersk 2
maintenance, outsourcing
    197, 198
management of contract 16,
    91, 104, 108, 115, 117–18,
    123, 171, 176, 178, 183,
    192, 193, 216–22, 223,
    224
management control, models
    of 28–9
managing services in-house
    38–40
marketing, outsourcing 4, 197,
    198, 234

market value of outsourcing 3–4

measurement of performance 42, 46–8, 78–9, 85, 98, 102, 112, 113–14, 115, 128, 134, 152, 171, 173, 174, 175, 177, 181–4, 190–91, 192, 194, 198, 200, 205–9, 225

media management, outsourcing 4, 5

Mellon Bank 21

memorandum of understanding 132–4

mergers 8, 11

methodology for outsourcing 6, 18, 88

Microsoft 145

Ministry of Defence (UK) 3, 112

monitoring 171, 174, 177, 225

N

NASA 36

National Rivers Authority 157, 162

negotiation
  of contract 79, 91, 95, 101–3, 133, 134, 136, 140, 142, 143, 180
  locked room method 101

O

objectives x, 8, 14, 15, 39, 46, 47, 48, 54, 57, 81, 90, 91, 92–5, 106, 111, 121, 122, 124, 133, 134, 137, 152, 156, 173–5, 176, 181, 184, 188, 192, 206, 207, 208, 218, 219, 220, 222, 223, 224

occupiers' liability 149

outputs 41–4, 49, 102, 109, 111, 206, 224

outsourcing
  administration 198, 203, 205, 206, 213, 232
  ancillary services 6, 26, 41, 229
  approaches to 6–8, 37–49, 52–76
  benefits of x, 6, 8, 11–12, 15, 17, 34, 37, 47, 70–71, 78, 88, 100, 113, 127, 129, 160, 164, 171, 181–4, 190, 193, 194, 198, 225, 226, 227
  boundaries of 55, 67, 78, 112, 222, 224; *see also* scope
  buildings maintenance 20, 41
  catering 5, 20, 35, 41, 190, 197, 198
  cleaning 5, 6, 35, 41, 140, 197, 198
  concept of 2–18
  customer service 4, 233
  debt management 5, 196, 198

outsourcing (*cont.*)
distribution 197, 198, 205, 206, 213, 235
engineering 20, 196, 198, 206, 229
estate management 5, 197, 198
facilities management 5, 20, 40, 41, 132, 197, 198, 203–6, 234
factoring 5, 196, 198
finance 35, 196, 198, 203, 205, 206, 213, 233
growth of 3, 4, 19–36
guidelines for 223–4
human resource management 4, 35, 196, 233
in the UK 4, 189–230
in the US x, 4, 152
information technology 4, 5, 20–21, 22–4, 35, 48, 86, 116–17, 132, 140, 143, 145, 159, 176, 190, 192, 196–8, 199, 200, 202–3, 204–6, 208, 211, 227, 229, 230, 232
investment management 196, 198
legal services 196, 198
maintenance 197, 198
marketing 4, 197, 198, 234
market value of 3–4
methodology for 6, 18, 88
media management 4, 5
payroll 5, 35, 196, 198

pension management 196, 198
problems with 12–16, 179–80, 223
property services 5, 197, 198
public relations 5, 196
reasons for 8–11, 44, 54–5, 198, 202, 213, 231
sales ledger 5
scope of 55, 67, 100, 173; *see also* boundaries
security 20, 35, 197, 198
site services 197, 198, 203, 205, 206, 208
spending on 4
strategic approach ix, 5, 13, 19, 20, 21, 26, 57, 127, 192, 223
transport 197, 198, 205, 206, 213, 235
warehousing 197, 198
Outsourcing Institute 9, 14
survey 231–5
Outsourcing World Summit 4
Oxford University Institute of Information Management 12

P

partnership 5, 30, 32, 45–6, 47, 115, 118, 132, 183, 220–22, 225
payment terms 148–9

payroll, outsourcing 5, 35, 196, 198
pensions 162
performance
  evaluation of 98, 108, 115, 117, 125, 181
  measurement of 42, 46–8, 78–9, 85, 98, 102, 112, 113–14, 115, 128, 134, 152, 171, 173, 174, 175, 177, 181–4, 190–91, 192, 194, 198, 200, 205–9, 225
  review of 81, 173, 177, 178, 193, 220, 224
  sanctions 139–40, 173, 175–6
planning x, 14, 15, 53, 75, 87, 88–105, 106, 156, 188, 192, 227
planning, transition 75, 104, 159–60, 172–3
post-contract verification 96, 114, 172
problems with outsourcing 12–16, 179–80, 223
property services, outsourcing 5, 197, 198
public relations, outsourcing 5, 196
public sector 170–71, 186, 195, 196
  New Zealand 22
  UK 22
purpose, corporate 31–2

Q

quality 11, 15, 42, 44, 54, 171, 177, 181, 182, 190, 191, 200, 202, 204, 206, 208, 209, 218, 219, 226, 228

R

reasons for outsourcing 8–11, 44, 54–5, 198, 202, 213, 231
reference sites 45, 83, 97, 99, 100, 123
relationship
  with customers 33–5, 36, 82
  with service provider 15, 44–6, 49, 78, 82, 95, 96, 106–8, 114, 115–18, 125–6, 131, 134, 165, 180, 193, 194, 214, 215, 217–18, 219, 220, 222, 224–5
reletting the contract 185–7
renegotiating the contract 141, 226
reporting 102, 145, 147–8, 224
request for proposals 123–5
research 53, 83–7, 93
resistance from employees 163–6
  overcoming 165–6
resources 10, 25, 32–3, 35, 80, 89, 90, 113–14, 147–8, 160, 231

review of performance 81,
  173, 177, 178, 193, 220,
  224
review, strategic 186–7
rewards 132, 184, 222, 225
risk analysis table 73–4
risks 8, 10, 25–6, 37, 73–4,
  90, 104, 122, 132, 134–6,
  144, 221, 222, 225, 231
Rolls-Royce 47, 116–17

S

Sainsbury's Bank 32
sales ledger, outsourcing 5
sanctions for poor performance 139–40, 173, 175–6
scope of outsourcing 55, 67,
  100, 173
Sears 14
security, outsourcing 20, 35,
  197, 198
selecting service provider 15,
  100, 106–30, 156
senior management support
  81, 91, 92, 99, 100, 106
sensitivity analysis 72–3
SERCO 3
service delivery manager 44,
  126–7, 176
service level agreement 5, 40,
  91, 96, 101–3, 128–9, 174,
  176, 180, 192, 209, 220,
  224
service provider
  financial viability of 144–6

relationship with 15, 44–6,
  49, 78, 82, 95, 96, 106–8,
  114, 115–18, 125–6, 131,
  134, 165, 180, 193, 194,
  214, 215, 217–18, 219, 220,
  222, 224–5
selecting 15, 100, 106–30,
  156
shortlisting 91, 98, 118
visits to 119–20
service specification 108–18,
  128, 181, 192, 223
shortlisting service providers
  91, 98, 118
Shreeveport 3, 6, 16, 18, 27,
  37, 41, 52, 59, 88, 91, 93,
  95, 109, 124, 156, 157,
  171, 185
survey 171, 189–230
SIA 19
Signet 38
site services, outsourcing 197,
  198, 203, 205, 206, 208
specification of requirement
  98, 100, 115, 117, 128, 224
spending on outsourcing 4
stakeholders 160, 165, 224
strategic approach to outsourcing ix, 5, 13, 19, 20,
  21, 26, 57, 127, 192, 223
strategic context 67–9
strategic review 186–7
strategic sourcing 37, 186
  concept of 26–30
  definition 26–7
subcontracting 5

suppliers, evaluation of 99,
100, 120–23
supply hierarchy 33–6

T

termination of contract 116,
139, 142
Thomas Cook 159
timescale 90, 96, 103, 113,
135, 173, 223
transition 91, 103–4, 107,
129, 152, 163, 166, 171–3,
177
transition plan 75, 104,
159–60, 172–3
transport, outsourcing 197,
198, 205, 206, 213, 235

U

University of Missouri 12
user satisfaction surveys 208,
225

V

vertical integration 9, 10
virtual organizations 2, 10,
229
visits to service providers
119–20

W

warehousing, outsourcing 197,
198
Warren Company 11